THE STARCHED BLUE SKY OF SPAIN

THE STARCHED BLUE SKY OF SPAIN

AND OTHER MEMOIRS

JOSEPHINE HERBST

Introduction by Diane Johnson

HarperCollins*Publishers*

"A Year of Disgrace" appeared in *The Noble Savage*, no. 2. "Yesterday's Road" appeared in *New American Review*, no. 3. "The Starched Blue Sky of Spain" appeared in *The Noble Savage*, no. 1.

THE STARCHED BLUE SKY OF SPAIN AND OTHER MEMOIRS. Copyright © 1991 by the Estate of Josephine Herbst. All rights reserved. Printed in the United States of America. No part of this book may be used or reproduced in any manner whatsoever without permission except in the case of brief quotations embodied in critical articles and reviews. For information address HarperCollins Publishers, 10 East 53rd Street, New York, NY 10022.

FIRST EDITION

Designed by Alma Orenstein

Library of Congress Cataloging-in-Publication Data

Herbst, Josephine, 1892–1969.
  The starched blue sky of Spain : and other memoirs / by Josephine Herbst.
    p. cm.
  ISBN 0-06-016512-X
  1. Herbst, Josephine, 1892–1969—Biography. 2. Novelists, American—20th century—Biography. 3. Journalists—United States—Biography. 4. Spain—History—Civil War, 1936–1939—Personal narratives. I. Title.
PS3515.E596Z47   1991
813'.52—dc20
[B]   90-55931

91 92 93 94 95 CC/HC 10 9 8 7 6 5 4 3 2 1

Contents

Introduction by Diane Johnson   vii

The Magicians and Their Apprentices   1

A Year of Disgrace   53

Yesterday's Road   99

The Starched Blue Sky of Spain   129

Introduction

In recent years, literary history has been something like archaeology, the unearthing of buried lives and reputations and forgotten works, especially of women. One of the most lustrous rediscoveries has been that of Josephine Herbst, in an admirable biography by Elinor Langer, begun four years after Herbst's death, in 1969, and published in 1983 under the title *Josephine Herbst: The Story She Could Never Tell.* The woman whom Langer had so narrowly missed knowing in life she found to have remained a troubling presence in the minds of everyone who had known her:

> whether it was because the woman was so poor and isolated and had no plumbing in her old stone farmhouse—a fact I was told with peculiar frequency—and they were uneasy about the degree of human assistance they had given or not given her; whether it was because she was publicly neglected and they did not sincerely respect her as a writer, much as they enjoyed her company; whether politics had torn them asunder and now they regretted it—this I could not tell.

However it had happened, Josephine Herbst's last years were blighted by the sulfurous taint that clings to people who outlive their celebrity. She was championed only by a few nostalgic or visionary friends—her executor, Hilton Kramer, for example, and Ted Solotaroff, the editor of these memoirs, who had originally published one of them in the *New American Review*. Despite Herbst's considerable body of work—novels, stories, memoirs, and journalism covering particularly tumultuous times from the twenties to the sixties, she had not even been mentioned in literary histories by influential critics like Edmund Wilson and Malcolm Cowley, and was sometimes listed in indexes of books about the period as "Mrs. John Herrmann."

Even poor and isolated, however, Josephine Herbst at the end of her life was still at work, and paradoxically it was then that she found her strongest voice. The four essays reprinted here ("The Magicians and Their Apprentices," "A Year of Disgrace," "Yesterday's Road," and "The Starched Blue Sky of Spain"), written in her last years, are unequaled by her fiction even at its finest. These memoirs have much of what must have been her personality—intense, sincere, intelligent, demanding. Her death was untimely, though she was seventy-six, for she had much left to say and do. She wanted to finish her memoirs, and she planned a series of stories that would have constituted an invaluable literary history of her period (she finished only one, "A Hunter of Doves," about Nathanael West). She had led a Literary Life, full of passionate discussions of Joyce or Schwitters or Cubism or Antheil. She was a friend of the famous writers of her day—of Hemingway, Dos Passos, Maxwell Anderson, Katherine Anne Porter. Maxwell Perkins was her editor. There were winter idylls snowed up with her young husband in a farmhouse, reading Shakespeare and writing. She turns up in accounts of the war in Spain, of prewar Germany, of the radical farm movement in the thirties, of the corollary persecutions of the McCarthy period. To her name clung the luster of commitment, compassion, and courage—in all, she had led very much the glamorous life of travel and famous friends that in her childhood in a little midwestern town she dreamed of having. Of course, she did her writing too—journalism, articles, and seven novels, all respectfully and widely reviewed. But in some sense the writing was a means to an end—the life she lived.

And it was only in her sixties that in turning to this life as a subject, she found her real tone. Because she had fallen under the influence of the serious political mood of the thirties, the brilliant satirist and novelist of manners in her had not been allowed to surface; but something of her natural Peacockian wit and edge had free rein in the essays. Where the political agenda of her novels seems a bit willed, stuck onto material that wants to wiggle out from under it, like a Band-Aid on a child's wet knee, the essays give a lively picture of this contrary and peculiar epoch and its characters. We observe Ford Maddox Ford's "imposing white walrus presence" as he sits with his feet in a tub, see Katherine Anne Porter's gingham curtains, meet crowds of young artists from the Midwest and South enjoying the artistic life of New York or Europe "as if it had never happened before, feeling ourselves actors in a rare moment, caught in a situation that would require not only flexibility but intensity of purpose. . . . You might not be a Dante; but Dante was dead."

Josephine Herbst herself was an earnest midwesterner, born in 1892 in Sioux City, Iowa, to a middle-class family on its way down (as she would come to see it), sinking into the proletariat as capitalism itself was widely said at the time to be about to sink and disappear. There was not, of course, much of a proletariat in Sioux City, though there were farmers. Her father kept the hardware store and sold farm implements. It was a female household. Her mother, a cultivated woman, was the force in the family, and Josephine had three sisters. Their mother hoped for great things for them, especially for Josie—for something "more" than marriage and children.

Though it was not common for women at this period, Josie went to college, first to the local college, then to the University of California at Berkeley, working her way through by teaching and taking other low-paying jobs. After Berkeley she went, as young Iowans still do, to New York, where, as an advanced, liberated young person, she had an affair: with the playwright Maxwell Anderson, a married man intending to stay married. When she became pregnant, she had an abortion, which remained as an emotional scar and perhaps a physical one, for she never had children.

To take her mind off her personal life, she went to Germany in 1922, living as a "dollar princess" in the inflationary economy and hectic strangeness of prewar Berlin, then to Paris, and it was there that she met John Herrmann, another American writer, a few years younger than she, whom she would in time marry and with whom she would live the romantic idyll of the isolated farmhouse and pass winters in Key West, in Hemingway's circle (cross, like the other wives, that the men spent so much time fishing). She and Herrmann went to a conference of revolutionary writers in Russia in 1930. In the bleak Depression of the thirties, they felt, as so many writers and intellectuals did, that something must be done about society, and Josie threw herself into political work, but also, now, wrote her three best novels, the saga of the Trexlers, based on her family: *Pity Is Not Enough* (1932); *The Executioner Waits* (1934); *Rope of Gold* (1937), recently republished as "The Rediscovered Trexler Trilogy." In 1937 she went to Spain to cover the events of the civil war.

Her marriage to John Herrmann had broken up in 1935. This seems to have been the major disappointment of her personal life. Among other relationships, she was to have two serious affairs with women. In view of this liberated eclecticism, it is interesting that in her work she never discusses sex, a telling reticence only in part explained by her generation and upbringing. Despite her reticence, she was all along passionately frank about such women's issues as marriage, abortion, menstruation, "female complaints," female powerlessness. "Women had been given the vote, but if they were now 'emancipated,' it was not through suffrage but by jobs, birth control, even Prohibition," she writes in "A Year of Disgrace," regarding issues of the twenties that would be set aside during the Second World War, to resurface in the 1960s. Elinor Langer discusses the impression *The Golden Notebook* made on Herbst when she read it at the age of seventy-one and saw in Lessing's forthright treatment of many of the questions that had concerned her, too, a more courageous and modern voice than her own. Yet her own novels were among the earliest to have strong heroines (as opposed to victim heroines), and her discussions of such topics as abortion must have seemed very advanced.

Given Herbst's feminism, what is striking in her accounts of her growing up is the genderlessness of her experience, and her relative lack of a sense of female constraints until she left home. One of the happiest memories of her childhood was a family camping trip to Oregon, where she "learned how to catch mud cats and cut them up for bait; how to cast a line in a trout stream"; how to catch a crab or cook an oyster—with little consciousness of what were conventional girls' activities. It was the same with intellectual influences. She would read Joyce and Anatole France, Stendhal and Lenin, with as much passion as the Brontës and George Sand evoked in her. As to role models, her mother was competent and free-spirited, and "even in our modest town we had women who set an example for a girl ambitious to go beyond the domestic circle. Our family doctor was married to a woman who was also a practicing physician. At the Unitarian Church . . . there were two women preachers." When she gets her first period, "I was amazed to discover myself of a vast company, exclusively female, who were regularly reminded in language of the blood of what they were. Not only my mother, my sisters, my teachers, but the Brontë girls, George Sand! The Queen of England! Was it a thistle or a rose? I could not say."

If as a child she had felt herself an undifferentiated person, of neither sex, at college she began to feel herself "a girl with the ambitions and aspirations of a boy," and in a strange episode, submitted to complicated and probably unwarranted gynecological surgery, ostensibly to correct the anatomy of her internal organs.

There is nowhere any discussion of her attraction to women, or perhaps only traces of it, as when she recalls the alluring transparent blouse of her Sunday school teacher, "revealing the ravishment of an embroidered 'corset cover' threaded with pink ribbons." In a letter to one of her woman lovers, she confesses to feeling "impotent," a word suggestive, perhaps, of her relatively androgynous or even masculine spirit.

Wanting at some level to be a man, or at least to have male privileges, she resented being excluded from the circles of the male intellectual left, which in common with the Communist Party had little interest in the concerns of women or even believed that to express them would be divisive and harmful to the interests of the (male) "masses." She wrote sarcastically to her friend Katherine Anne Porter about being excluded from a "wordy feast" of political talk that John Herrmann was invited to "over beer, as you might know, . . . full of a masculine importance you and I will never know, alas. . . . I told Mister Herrmann that as long as the gents had bourgeois reactions to women they would probably never rise very high in their revolutionary conversations but said remarks rolled off like water." Her tone is strikingly similar to that of Meridel Le Sueur, Tillie Olsen, and other radical women of the period, bitter but surprisingly resigned. Men cannot change. Though she saw the tension between male intellectuals and ambitious New Women, she was not without a Victorian ability stoically to make a virtue of necessity. Things were at least better than before. "If a fine martial spirit existed between the sexes, it was a tonic and a splendor after so much sticky intermingling and backboneless worship of the family and domesticated bliss," she stoutly insists.

Katherine Anne Porter comes up again and again in her recollections. Porter and Herbst were friends, at one time close, took different turnings, and eventually, if not enemies, they were no longer friends. Elinor Langer reveals that in the fifties, Porter would denounce Herbst to the FBI. She had let Herbst down at other times too—for instance, when she failed to deliver a promised review of Josie's novel *Satan's Sergeants*, though this wounding omission may in retrospect be seen to have been an act of charity on Porter's part, for it was not Herbst's strongest work. The two women afford an instructive comparison, two views of the artist, especially the woman artist; while male artists through art escape from the workaday office or ditch-digging imperatives of being men, women are seldom freed from the exigencies of womanhood. The often-married Porter would trade on her beauty (or was perhaps its victim); Herbst essentially rejected a conventional female life. Big-hearted, committed, the less talented, homelier, and more vulnerable of the two, she was made to suffer, if suffer she did, by life, not art. Her writing reveals a nature more needy than Porter's. Her relationships were her sorrows. The beautiful, talented, disaffected Porter—the greater writer and perhaps lesser person—seemed to have cared more for her art. It may be that Herbst has more to say to us today.

Unlike Porter, Josephine Herbst kept faith with an early ideal, shared with many writers of the time, of a literary life and of a literary community. The literary life seemed to mean, for her, that literature was in some sense true, was to be an operative force in daily life, and that its practice was therefore sacred, something for which hardships should be endured. Again and again, especially in her essay "A Year of Disgrace," we are given a vivid sense of how her commitment to literature shaped her life. Books were like food to the young Herrmanns, as to their friends. During the snow-bound months in the country, they wrote in the day—she in the kitchen to keep her eye on the cooking—and in the evenings, to the light of "the Aladdin oil lamp cast[ing] a mellow glow the color of a ripe pear," they "retreated" to nineteenth-century literature, reading aloud to each other, with a keg of hard cider at hand. Her apparently simple description of the operation of great writing on the imagination of another writer is one of the most interesting and precise to be found of the elusive phenomenon of inspiration:

> There were times, when we came to a work I already knew, when I let the words flow over me like water, hearing and not hearing, while some other self burrowed in the dark, sorting out those thoughts that were so manifold and evanescent, or reviewed the past, yesterday or the year before, or speculated on the present. Everything fused, fleetingly, in a flux and ferment, fired by a spark from the words being spoken while you waited, expectant, for the passage that jubilantly intoxicates the heart.

Books were not only nourishment; they were the business of their daily lives. Literary gossip, literary politics, and literary friendships—what might today be called "support groups"—these took a lot of their time. Young writers of their set kept up with the avant-garde periodicals, like *transition* or *This Quarter*, and dutifully smuggled copies of *Ulysses* from France. They found apartments for each other and read each other's work. This sense of literary community was to remain important to Herbst even when she had reason no longer to believe in it.

Where most of us revise the past as we move forward through the present, Josephine Herbst retains something like total recall for all the visual details of what her circle wore and ate and did.

> I would be sitting before my typewriter, and an entire scene from a past time would be suspended before my eyes, enclosed within some magic circle, something apart from any of the life that had gone before or that might ever come again.

Above all, her descriptions of the artistic *Zeitgeist* fascinate today. If total recall is rare, it is far rarer to be able to capture the fleeting climate of thought of a period past in a lovely image, as when, speaking of the twenties, she notes:

> If we had abandoned the safe lives our parents had fancied so valuable, we seemed to have gained an insight into the creative fissures of the world. The fires and smoke steamed up from volcanoes, old and new. What had Baudelaire *really* said? Was Poe a phony? Stendhal, newly translated in the twenties, became a contemporary, a young man speaking for the age.

Above all, she challenges the received accounts of such glorified historical events as the Spanish Civil War or the climate of post-revolutionary Russia. The reader knows it is she who is telling the truth when she says that the war was not all gallantry and justice or that there was no such thing as the twenties: "The decade simply falls apart upon examination into crumbs and pieces which completely contradict each other in their essences." Then she goes on to give an eyewitness account that notes all the contradictions; one, moreover, that seems relatively untainted by revisionist egotism. Where the myth, and hence the past, of, say, Hemingway (a particular subject of fascination with her) has continued to be altered, Herbst stands, it seems, apart from herself, an almost disembodied and unusually detailed recording sensibility that will brook no distortion.

Her belief in literary community seems in part a function of the way she lived, hospitably and openly, and in part an aspect of the belief in collective action that influenced her politics. She was often deceived by her optimism into misjudging the loyalty and commitment of other writers to some cause she believed in, but she was never deceived for long. A special note of disapproval is reserved for someone she perceives as putting himself forward at the expense of the collective good, like Hemingway when she thinks that he is "playing a lone hand in Paris." When, at the writers' congress in Russia, she hears an American writer praise a work without mentioning that he was the author of it, she leaves the room in disgust.

Herbst thought that writing should be politically committed and was thought of as a political writer. In a speech in 1935 on the opening night of the first American Writers' Congress (organized by the Communist Party), proclaiming herself inspired by the growing radicalism she had seen among the American working classes, she declared: "this is a marvelous time to be alive." But like other serious writers of the period, when it came to wrestling her material into forms and subjects prescribed for revolutionary writing, she began to demur, saying eventually that she was "tired of being asked to do things the way I was asked to speak . . . yes, they had to have a woman so long as they had a negro and a worker." She had wanted to be wanted for her writing.

Her attitude of detachment, even disaffection, had been much the same at the writers' congress with John Herrmann in 1930. Instead of being about writing, as she had hoped, the congress was political. She was disappointed because the serious writers she had hoped for were not there ("did they hide?"), and she was bored by the lecturing, depressed by the idea that housewives were to be rescued "from kitchen slavery to work in factories of shiny glass." And she was embarrassed by the "gloomy three" American delegates who never went to any parties ("dogma to them was the needed arm, not anathema"). She says in "Yester-

day's Road" that "those days were best before the delegations swept in."

"Yesterday's Road," her disapproving backward look
at the thirties, is written in a tone of injured patriotism after
she was fired from a responsible wartime information job in
1943 and then actively persecuted in the fifties. It is undoubtedly sincere, though how much unconscious revision
it contains is hard to say. Like most writers, Herbst tends
to put herself in a good light—one of the few privileges of
authorship, and some would say the point of it. Her remarkable—even curious—ability to move forward and backward
in history, recapturing and contrasting opposing states of
mind, is never more in evidence than when, writing about
the writers' congress years later, at a time when she was
under a cloud for disloyalty, the cloud did not prevent her
from making a good bit of justified fun at the American
propagandists running the wartime agency, for their at-
tempts to undermine the German soldiers' morale, while
Germany was engaged in the most grisly crimes the world
has known, with taunts about the fidelity of their wives.

It seems clear, not only from her own account of her
radical years but from the letters of the same period, that she
was never comfortable with the sexism, conformism, and
dogmatism of the left even though she was committed to it
and to the idea of revolution, a conflict of principle and
temperament that may well have produced in her a kind of
paralysis and was destructive to her fiction. She said, and her
biographer affirms, that she was never a member of the
Communist Party. Her executor says she was nonetheless a
Stalinist. It was a choice of isms she might have thought
unnecessary; the truly detached have a kind of hardhearted
consistency, such as might well have muted her objections
to the Stalin purges. A middle-western, small-town Unitar-

ian with no immediate immigrant connections might easily find the idea of communism interesting, for the Midwest is a region with a tradition of prairie radicalism and a history of experimental communistic societies (the Mennonites, New Harmony, etc.) and liberal or progressive politicians (Stevenson, Anderson, McGovern, McCarthy, to think of a few recent ones). Iowans had an abstract belief in social justice because social justice was not difficult to envisage in the little towns and farms that, though poor, were already essentially classless—middle-class communities of which some members were less poor than others.

The Iowa of Josephine Herbst's childhood (like, probably, the Iowa of today) also had no real hereditary connection to the isms of Eastern Europe, whether Marxism or Freudianism; it had a real antipathy to regimentation and to systems of thought demanding orthodoxy and dogma. These were aversions Herbst shared. On the prairie, with all its cultural roots in the genteel nineteenth century of England, Germany, and Scandinavia, isms did pass through, notably in the farm movement; but in the spacious farmland and sleepy towns, the social convulsions that were engulfing masses elsewhere must have been hard to envisage. ("The Communist press wrote jargon for 'workers' most of the time, and in the Midwest they had no circulation worth a damn," Josie wrote.) This seems to be the paradox of Herbst's political life—a committed heart and an Iowan skepticism.

All along, Josie's Marxism seems to have been temperamental, based more on her nature than on social philosophy: "One Me, a jaundiced eye on Progress, was a gloomy prognostician; the other, a congenital cricket, ready to chirp, 'while there's life, there's hope. . . .' "

Herbst was gregarious, and she liked being where

things were happening—hence the trip to Spain, which she recounts in her evocative essay "The Starched Blue Sky of Spain." It was her staunch inability to be dishonest that kept her from writing about Spain just after her visit there during the civil war, because "There was one thing you couldn't do when you came back from Spain. You couldn't begin to talk in terms of contradictions. . . . What was wanted was black or white." Rather than distort, she would set the subject aside. When she came to write about it, she captured with absolute freshness, after more than twenty years, the contradictions of the civil war: the matter-of-factness of the fighters of the Spanish front contrasting with the romantic bravado of the writers who hung out at the Hotel Florida, assembled to prey on the war (like herself, as she never forgets). And she pillories everybody else's contradictions along with her own. Hemingway wanted to be "*the* war writer of his age, and he knew it and went toward it," yet he lived luxuriously and dined on partridge. "There was a kind of splurging magnificence about Hemingway at the Florida, a crackling generosity whose underside was a kind of miserliness. He was stingy with his feelings to anyone who broke his code, even brutal." In her description of Hemingway in Spain lies a clue, perhaps, to the origin of her preoccupation with this old friend and fellow midwesterner: "Part of his exuberance came from the success of his love affair [with Martha Gellhorn]. But even his love affair was not exactly a benign influence in a wartime hotel. The corks popping were not for you."

Even then, in Spain, a characteristic trick of her consciousness, experiencing the present in terms of the past, operated continuously. Wandering in a village, she sees the craters of bombs, which remind her of swallows' nests along the Missouri River. The magnificent old strong Spanish women railing at the enemy "reduced my memory of fashionable ladies back home, with their little stereotyped lavender curls and their mincing high heels, to a parody of a potential they had forfeited." Often the memory of a work of art will be part of her experience of the present moment. In a little Spanish schoolroom, packed with people of different nationalities, she thinks of the Quaker Hicks's paintings of "The Peaceable Kingdom"; and some Yugoslavians singing remind her of Fra Angelico. Thus she weaves quadruple layers of consciousness—the then, the before then, the now, and the analogy in art—and it is this that accounts for the richness and the evocativeness of her writing.

The passionate intensity of her observation seems her special gift and an aspect of her temperament, and her temperament, in turn, seems very much a product of her midwestern childhood. The map of world climate zones represents the climate of Iowa as "Mongolian Steppe," a bitterly cold and ruthlessly hot belt that encompasses all the land from Iowa northward through Canada across the top of the world to the steppes of Russia. Other midwesterners have recounted their longing for escape from this inland desert and their sense, so Chekhovian, that the real world exists elsewhere. Herbst herself makes explicit the connection to Chekhov:

> all those dreamy Russian girls, who strolled away from tea tables on the sunny verandas . . . to moon under the lime trees, watching the far horizon across the flat steppes—so like our prairies—for the puff of dust that would announce the approaching troika with its ravishing stranger: how *true* they were! . . . no wonder the Three Sisters, when we finally came upon them, haunted us and stiffened our resolve to get beyond helpless yearning to the Real Thing.

xxi

Looking back at her work and her career, it seems that her motive force, and even her intrinsic subject, was never politics so much as this experience of being a midwesterner, or rather of escaping from the Midwest, and yearning for the culture of the great world. From childhood it had seemed to her, as to Hemingway, as to thousands of prairie children,

> that we were stranded in the middle of a country that offered its most tempting gifts to the people who lived on the eastern seaboard, "back East," where my parents had been born and raised, or "out West" on the Pacific, where more fortunate relatives had been safely transported beyond our own barren middle ground. In Iowa you didn't have a chance to see a mountain or to hear the ocean roar.

Taken as a child to Oregon to visit relatives, she had her first sight of the ocean: "If I remember it as if it were yesterday, it's because of the shivering excitement; not only the goose-flesh of seeing old ocean but because I had been named to stand and wonder." It was of culture

> that you had dreamed in the midwest town before the war when the sky had pressed above your head like a burnished brass bowl and the long secretive dark express trains zipped into the horizon . . . You had dreamed of it as surely as you had dreamed of love. A book told you it was so, long before you had the chance to prove it, and when some knowing librarian, seeing you flounder in the bookstacks, had put into your hand books beyond your years to prove to you, beyond the shadow of a doubt, that explosive, wonderful, witty talk existed somewhere as surely as it did in the pages of *The Way of All Flesh, Sanine* [*sic*], or *Madame Bovary.*

Like Hemingway, with whom she seemed to feel a special kinship and rivalry, she found the great world and embraced it with a sense of wonder she never lost.

When she tried the great world, however, she not only had to contend with being a woman; she also had to contend with the cultural dominion of the East, its tendency not to take seriously either women or these yokels, as James T. Farrell complained ("in the East, and especially in New York, there . . . are those—far from few—who think that if a story is set in, say, South Dakota, it cannot be as important as a story set in New York"). In fact, all the major writers of the period were, finally, from the Midwest (or the South); but unlike the southerners, the midwesterners tended to set their stories far from home. Most of them, indeed, went far from home; they were a natural class of expatriates—Hemingway, Fitzgerald, Lewis, Cather—and these were the writers Herbst felt connected to and competitive with. It was clear to her and to the other outsiders "that what was going on in the world wasn't going to be decided by the [New York] literati anyhow. That's why I was always leaving for Germany, Cuba, Mexico, Latin America, the Midwest, and Spain." It is significant that she lists the Midwest with other foreign countries. "It would take years to value the long shadows on the grass, the smell of homemade bread, the hum of telegraph wires in the winds of an empty prairie," she wrote in "A Year of Disgrace." Come to value it she did, and to understand how it informed her writing and her life.

There is a gentle but pervasive note of envy in all her work, which suggests that in her life some ambition or plan had not turned out as she meant it to, some hunger remained unsatisfied. When writing against the grain, Josephine Herbst could write badly, as in her story "A Hunter of

Doves," a (nonetheless fascinating) reminiscence of Nathanael West, with its trace of malice and its tortured sentences ("Even the persons at the bar signified by their scars
that they had suffered on some desert isle of the spirit not
so remote from that abandoned spot where Bartram [West]
had planned to disenchant his victims in the novel he never
lived to complete," to choose a sentence at random). Her
novels suffer from a surplus of characters, and in her com-
pulsion to make them all cogs in the great march of history,
she often cuts them off just as they are about to speak most
feelingly. She shirks the scenes of drama of individual life;
people are born or die in paragraphs of which they are not
the subject.

But in her last essays, things had begun to come into
perspective, and hers was a remarkable perspective, honed
in remarkable times. Her criticism of the writing of the
fifties seems even more true in the climate of today's fiction
(which, as someone said, is about shopping and its conse-
quences):

> material prosperity can never answer the questions,
> why do we live, what does it mean? . . . It takes a true
> writer to show us what has been missing in our
> lives. . . . What has a writer to say if he agrees that this
> is the best of all possible worlds and all of our major
> problems have been solved on a miracle time belt of
> endless prosperity?
>
> What seems to be missing in a good deal of con-
> temporary writing is a sense of the world. The world
> around us. For some time we have had so many writers
> trailing their own nervous systems, premonitions, fan-
> tasies, and horrors that perhaps the time has come to dig
> up man, the guilty worm, and see him in relation to an
> actual world. . . . If past history is any guide, the present

phase that tends to the compulsive presentation of people as isolated moral atoms without any sensible relation to society or the ideas of their time ought to have departed before this.

She never admitted to being wrong about what writing should be about, and indeed she probably was not wrong. We still live in a time that needs someone like Josephine Herbst to remind us of the uses of art and the meaning of a literary life.

DIANE JOHNSON

The Magicians and Their Apprentices

WHEN I WAS SIX YEARS OLD, my mother took her four daughters on a reduced-fare jaunt to Oregon. Teddy Roosevelt was our President, but he meant nothing to me. I was still stuck with McKinley, our martyr. Our street had gone into mourning, and my older sisters had paraded me past the windows of our block. Every window displayed a lithographed image of the grave, smiling man, now dead by the hand of a forgotten assassin. Our house had the largest picture of any in our row, draped in a long black crape veil, which had once been the widow's veil of my grandmother.

We lived in Sioux City, Iowa, and we might have been dropped accidentally by some great auk on a transcontinental flight, so unreasonable it seemed that we were stranded in the middle of a country that offered its most tempting gifts to the people who lived on the eastern seaboard, "back East," where my parents had been born and raised, or "out West" on the Pacific, where more fortunate relatives had been safely transported beyond our own barren middle ground. In Iowa you didn't have a chance to see a mountain or to hear the ocean roar. And before that enchanted summer, I had never seen white ocean sand or known what it was to sit on it when scorching hot from a strong sun or that you could fill an empty bottle with hot sand and pour it down the open front of your blouse to flow in a tickling trickle over the hourglass of your ribs and thighs until it filled your bloomers to bursting and then slowly leaked away past the rubber band above the knees to seep like water into sand.

We rode for three days and nights in a wonderful train called a tourist Pullman, where the seats were upholstered in a straw-colored matting and smelled of hay, like the matting on the floors of our bedrooms at home when the sun burned. Every one of the passengers in our coach had a big basket of food, for there was no diner. At the back of the car was an upright stove with two burners, where my mother made hot cocoa for her brood and a stout woman wearing a stylish shirtwaist of pink-striped cotton fried eggs. The porter was our friend, setting up a little table for us to eat on and to play dominoes on when it got too dark to look out the window. Everyone on the train was a fascinating stranger. A young man with a violin serenaded us after we had crawled into our bunks; the two older girls, who were fourteen and twelve, slept upstairs, while my mother and her two youngest slept in a chummy heap below; the youngest was three. There was a gents' room and a ladies' room, with an aisle between, but at the other end of the car, near the stove, there was a tap for drinking water and a towel to wipe the hands. An old man introduced me to the amenities of life by delicately wetting the tips of his fingers as I wiped my own hands and informing me, in what I took to be gospel truth, that two who wiped their hands on the same towel simultaneously would be friends forever. But everyone

4

seemed to want to be friends forever. An old German couple from Milwaukee had brought a big hamper crammed with crocks of fresh apple butter, long sausages, great round loaves of bread, whole chickens, a ham. Because my mother acted as their translator when the conductor came through, we got big wedges of cheese, the legs and wings of a fat hen.

All day we sat with our noses glued to the windows as the incredible panorama unwound itself: plains sprouting wheat; plains sprouting stones; mountains rough and wild. Once my mother roused her two youngest at dawn: "Look, sheep!" As we looked out on a bleak Montana plain inhabited by a flock of stones, one stone moved, then another. A black shape reared, and we saw a dog's frenzy; the heap of stones got up and walked. Once we saw a bison with head down, lonely and frantic, stirring up spurts of dust as it raced toward the distant mountains. Long, stringy waterfalls slid like crystal glass down the sides of giant cliffs; rivers ran snaky green far below our valiant locomotive, which, humanly energetic, panted and puffed, scattered red sparks, and, in stations, stood docile, sweating steam and heaving passionately for breath. In Portland, we left our sleeper, bought a box of fat juicy strawberries, and ate them on the train to Salem.

We had seven cousins, two uncles, two aunts, and an old grandmother, tiny and straight as a blade of grass, wearing a starched lavender dress to match the veins in her hands. Even her blue eyes had the look of lavender; she was a wonder to behold. She lived alone in a white house sitting in the midst of pear and plum trees. The pears spurted juice when you bit them; the plums were purple and shiny, and we dried them on a big sheet in the sun to take back home as prunes. Then one day we made another trip, in my uncle's wide three-seated carryall drawn by the spanking

5

team of horses, Bess and Kate. Seven children, three adults, packed themselves in, tight-wedged but happy. The hired girl, Barbara, set out ahead, riding with the pack wagon, which held all the stuff we would need for two months of camping at Neskowin on the great Pacific.

It was noon when we left Salem on our celestial journey, and we didn't get to Neskowin until afternoon of the following day. At night we sheltered in a big barn where the loft was crammed with clover hay; when you spread your blanket out to sleep, the hay was springy beneath you; it was like a featherbed but more ticklish and sweeter. Below, the friendly horses clumped their oats and gulped. The neighbor cows rustled, breathed, and thudded on the plank floor spread with straw. When it was still dark, our enthusiastic uncle roused us with "All hands on deck!" We piled out to see a bright glow in the valley, where a campfire was mounted by a huge coffeepot and a big pan of eggs frying. The horses were led to the watering trough; the farmer and his son, with shiny milk pails, took over the barn; you could hear the musical tinkle of milk squirting into the pails. Standing around the fire, we munched eggs on bread, sipped coffee heavy with milk. To the east, the mountains showed firm against the silvery sky as the sun rose; but toward the west, the range of humps loomed dark as giant slugs, which we must pass over before we dipped down to the ocean.

All the children were ordered to walk up the mountain to save Bess and Kate. It was in the days before parents were terrorized by their children, and the adults rode serenely in state. The air, warmed by the rising sun, smelled of pine and blackberries. Under the Douglas firs, you could see the tall spikes of flowering foxgloves. On the other side of the mountain, the children heaved aboard the carryall. Now for the last dash past trout streams and tumbling waterfalls where, our uncle lectured, shouting backward from his front seat, the noble salmon made his leap, spurting up and up until his sides oozed blood, until at last he hit on the great arc to send him soaring above the falls to the pools beyond. What man could ever hope to rival such a leap! "Man can dive, nose downward, but whoever saw one leap over falls from below!"

Admonishing, sniffing, pointing, roaring, laughing, our uncle piloted us through leafy tunnels, above gorges, and, suddenly yelling, "Whoa, Bess, whoa, Kate," brought the team to a shuddering standstill. Turning, he yelled to my mother on the back seat, "Now we're coming to her. Around the next bend, you'll see old ocean. Get Josie up, let her stand up so she can get her first view of old ocean!" My mother got me up, holding to my skirts, and now the team moved on, slowly, and rounded the bend. "There she is," roared my uncle, "there she rolls from shore to distant shore." And miraculously, you heard her first, a deep slow lion's roar. Then, following my uncle's pointed whip, you saw her, lying in a long reach beyond the palest humps of sand, the breakers prancing in, foaming and rearing in splendor. If I remember it as if it were yesterday, it's because of the shivering excitement; not only the gooseflesh of seeing old ocean but because I had been named to stand and wonder. Bursting with pride, I stood braced by my mother's hand, a crazy red felt hat on my head, which was called a Napoleon hat in the fashion of that day, for indeed it had been modeled after the one worn in pictures of the little corporal sitting astride his horse, looking down at the smoke and the gore and the victory. My uncle, drunk with joy, orated as he drove on, "Roll on, thou deep and dark blue ocean, roll!"

7

We struck sand, and the wheels of the carryall glided silently as the runners of a sleigh. The campsite was in view of the ocean but sheltered by a pine grove, where tall ferns spilled in fountains of green. There were two big tents erected over new sweet-smelling pine planks. One was for my mother and her tribe; one for my uncle and his. Between, there was a dining and kitchen tent. The tents were a golden brown, and in the early morning, as I lay in bed, the light coming through had the color of buckwheat honey.

This was a summer for lore beyond books. Your hands and feet learned more than they had ever known they could do: how to catch mud cats and cut them up for bait; how to cast a line in a trout stream; how to dig your hands in oozy mud after the clam had squirted the signal of his little geyser. How to wait on the tide and how to find sea urchins and small fronds and ferns of sea moss in quiet pools. How to pry the rock oyster from his stony bed and how to cook him. How to catch a crab without getting pinched. How to walk barefoot on a slippery fallen log across the fiery sparkle of a tumbling mountain brook. How to stand still when you saw a deer. How to sit still around the campfire and listen to the gorgeous talk of grownups, who lived in their world, and you in yours, neither troubling to be pals with the other but only good friends.

It was a summer to remember not just for the new things your hands and feet discovered but for the glitter it offered of some distant beyond. There was someone's beyond behind you, and a beyond to come to pass, and this interlude was the curious glowing union of past and present, promises and reality. The grownups were the magicians, the children their apprentices.

It was at night, in the light of the big campfire of driftwood, where the burning splinters fell in sparks the

8

color of the rainbow or shot into tiny sulfurous spurts or foundered in pools of verdigris green, that the magicians and the apprentices played their true roles. For the circle was so gently relaxed, some sitting on rugs, some lying down and extending hands or feet toward the blaze, that a child of six could feel as detached as a bit of moss in a pool now covered by the tide. The very sound of the ocean and the sight of the sky, where the stars were bright buoys floating on their own watery deep, made you feel gently suspended in water, rocking in the vast hammock of the night. The voices of the grownups, slow, sometimes quietly breaking into laughter, communing over things dead and gone, remembering when my uncle and my mother were boy and girl together in a big family of other boys and girls, now scattered or dead, cast long lines backward in time and across a continent. *There* became *here* and *then* was *now*. The magicians might have been casting lines across an ocean covering buried towns and farms, so dreamlike was the world they called to life, so haunting the images, so watery the night, so true the history that branched its coral islands to you, by right, because it had belonged to them.

Strange names of towns burst like sparks of dying wood. A dead aunt once more played the piano on Arch Street in Philadelphia, and the wild boy who went south to Georgia sent home a bunch of bananas to hang at the top of the stairs. The red bird sang in his gilded cage, and the mockingbird died. Once more the faithful dog Rebbie begged for bread spread with smearcase and apple butter. And against the glow of the fire, the flesh of your bare toes became rosy luminous; the delicate dark skeleton showed stiff as the charred twigs of a burning bush.

•　•　•

9

If anyone had told me in 1930 that there was a connection between the trip John Herrmann and I were about to make to Russia and that first journey over the mountains to the ocean rolling from shore to distant shore, I would have mocked at the notion. I did not even see much of a connection between the house we now lived in, beside a brook, in the countryside of Pennsylvania, and that other, bigger stone house, some twenty miles away, south of Allentown, where my mother's family had lived through countless births and deaths for generations. What I would have recognized was that the world of the onetime magicians was breaking up.

The magicians were dead or about to die. My mother had died in 1925, after my return from a three-year stay in Europe. My father had died during the Wall Street crashes in the late fall of 1929. My uncle who had christened me with the wonders of old ocean had come to see us in the summer of 1930. A slender old man in dapper gray, he had traveled east from Oregon for the fiftieth anniversary of his graduating class in Philadelphia. He was proud of his role as a good after-dinner speaker—he got a lot of practice, it appeared, back home—and he was proud of his success as a businessman. He had been a druggist and then moved into the wholesale drug trade and finally, through "wise investments," had stacked it up until he was now president of a very solid bank. He had handsome engraved personal cards with his name and his title as bank president, and during his brief week with us he passed out his cards wherever he got the opportunity—at filling stations and to the hardware merchant from whom he had bought a flashlight. Making sharp deals had got him where he was, but there came a moment late one afternoon, as he sat looking over some old family letters I had inherited from my mother, when he shook his head and said: "Josie, I wouldn't walk across the street for a deal in any shape or form. No, sir, the biggest deal in the world wouldn't tempt me."

He was sitting opposite me, at a long trestle table made of pinewood two hundred years old. Its surface was satiny, beautiful and uneven, and one of his hands would move occasionally in an involuntary caress across the surface of the wood. His hands had come to look like my grandmother's the only time I had ever seen her, and when he lifted his head to look at me, I saw that he also now bore a striking resemblance to my mother as she had looked the weeks before she died. At Neskowin they had not resembled one another at all; my uncle was already bald, and the little fringe of hair at the base of his skull, though red like my mother's hair, appeared faded in comparison to her bright crown. Now the fringe was white, and so was his neat mustache, clipped in the fashion of the successful executive. Both of them had the fair skin of the redhead, and in hearty middle age both had been delightfully rounded, juicy, bursting with energy and shiny with life. With old age, the roundness had melted down without losing its firm quality; the delicate skeleton made hollows and arcs in their high foreheads, showed in the cheekbones and the caverns of the eyes, but the eyes, a cornflower blue, looked out with the eager, open expression of a child. My uncle turned these eyes upon me now, and I was struck with their likeness to my mother's. His cheeks, too, were flushed with an inner excitement as hers used to be, after I had come home and before she knew she was to die, when she had tried to draw out for me the meanings of a lifetime and to make some kind of continuity to pass on to her child. But there had been certain aspects, even then, too painful to talk about; he and I could only bring ourselves to talk about my younger sister—my closest companion for twenty years—as a young, ardent girl; she was already dead.

There was a look in my uncle's eyes, as he stared at me almost unseeingly, that seemed to hold all the questions of a lifetime. He held in one hand a letter, yellowed and beautiful with a script that no one writes anymore; it had been the last letter ever written by his father, who had died when my uncle was eight weeks old. The letter was to the older brothers of my uncle, who had been sent with their sisters to the house of an aunt in Bethlehem when the baby was born. The letter was about the new baby—my uncle— whom the father called "a little bunny rabbit." My uncle wanted this letter and asked for it now with the kind of trepidation of someone who is demanding to share an estate not intended for him.

"Take it," I said. "You can have it. It really belongs to you." "You mean it?" he said, gaping at me, his mouth slightly open. "Yes, of course." He folded it carefully, put it in his pocket. Sat for a moment, thoughtfully, caressing the table. And because I was very much moved, I hardened myself, looked at him stonily, thinking of the sacrifices my mother and her sisters had made for him and his brothers at a time when the boys of a family were expected to carry all its hopes and fortune. How different my mother's life had been, how hard its declining years, while my uncle's had seemed only to soar, up and up. Yet here he sat now, like my mother, at the end of the road. He knew it, and I knew he knew it, and he knew that I knew. It was one of those moments. He smiled, asked in a wondering, small boy's voice, "What's it all about? Do you know?" And once more the arrogance of youth protected me; I thought to myself: When it's my time I'll know more. I wouldn't be asking questions of someone forty years younger. But I had the kindness not to answer him like that; my mother moved into me and made my voice gentle. I said, "But you've had a wonderful life." He stared at the table, moving his hand as if upon a map that would show clearly the rivers, the brooks, the mountains where the brooks had their source, the great plains washing down to the sea. He sighed. "It's not enough. I don't know any of the answers or what it all means."

In the lapel of his coat was a round button. It had been presented to him by the Rotarians in Tokyo when he was making a trip with his wife around the world. I kept looking at it now, for to look at him was painful, and seeing it, I was reminded of the hotel room in New York where I had come to see my aunt and uncle two years before, on their return from the voyage. My aunt, a fine, big woman in a great upholstery of lush flesh, with a sage, beautiful face and glowing dark eyes, had told me that "Papa isn't interested in business anymore." I had thought to myself, cynically: No wonder; he's made it. Then she had gone on: "What he's interested in is brotherhood; he only cares about International Rotary and things like that." It had caught me, for just a moment; I thought of myself as an internationalist too. But a second later mockery set in, and I disdained an internationalism that spoke in terms of business enterprise and where, to my notion, "getting together" mean brotherhood for the big deal. Now, however, looking at my uncle, I was ashamed of my earlier opinion. It seemed to me both true and superficial, and that way down under his view and my view, there was another stratum, holding its meanings, secret and aloof, from both of us.

But there was not time to go after what might be concealed treasure; I had to push it aside. My uncle wanted to take a last look at the old Easter Egg. It had been one of my mother's most cherished relics. Of a dark garnet color, it bore the date marked in white, 1809, and had been dyed by her grandfather when a boy. Once a year, on Easter, it was taken out of its cotton nest in an old sugar bowl for my mother's four daughters to admire. We weren't allowed to touch it; only to look. I brought it out now and carefully unwrapped it. It had the shine of old dark wood, and the white lettering had mellowed to old ivory. My uncle was in raptures. "It ought to be kept under glass," he said. "To keep the air out. If you did that it would last forever." His blue eyes were popping with excitement, and as he leaned forward, gaping, he reminded me of a baby in its crib, suddenly seeing the dangling colored ball.

"Why don't you take it home with you," I said unexpectedly. I was surprised at myself. "You can put it under glass. I never would." He stared at me. "You really mean it?"

"Of course. Take it. I've had it since my mother died, and we had it for years before that. Now it's your turn." I felt as expansive as my uncle might have been allowed to feel if he had endowed a youngster with a scholarship to college. "Josie," he said solemnly, "I'll prize it. It will be my most treasured possession. When I look at it," he went on, lapsing into platitudes, "and think of all the living people dead and gone, and this egg, this fragile *thing*, has outlived them all!" And for a second, his eyes went wild, racing around the room as if to call the dead and gone from behind the Welsh dresser or to come out from hiding in the corner cupboard.

Then he got up, straightened himself, buttoned his open coat, and stood like the director of a board meeting, which, back home, he undoubtedly had been. "We'll have to call this off," he said briskly, as he might say closing a business deal, and it was with relief that I saw his public manner take precedence over his private revelations, for I wanted him to get going, to be on his way. We were to drive him to Philadelphia that afternoon, taking in a few last places where he still hoped he might find one of his boyhood friends or the Gerhardt sisters, his cousins, one of whom had been a "raving beauty." The car we were to drive him in was an old Model T number, which we had bought from Allen Tate for twenty-five dollars two years before, when the Tates drove up from the South on their way to Paris, leaving their cherished "Old 97" at our door. They had used it during their visits to old battlefields of the South as part of the research Allen had been doing for a work about Stonewall Jackson. I told my uncle this now, as we all three packed into the front seat; it was a tight squeeze.

"Our family," began my uncle sententiously, "happens to be pathetically barren of military heroes. We are a peace-loving race, Josie, and there is that legend about our great-great-grandfather who hid in the hay the day a daughter was born to his wife and the soldiers came to get him to join up for our American Revolution and prodded the hay with pitchforks. One of my girls got pretty worked up about our lack of war heroes, seeing the length of time we had been around. Wanted to belong to the Daughters of the American Revolution but couldn't find the missing link." He burst into a hearty guffaw, and his face flushed bright crimson. Suddenly I remembered the story my mother had reluctantly told me. She had been so chagrined for her brother, how he had refused to buy bonds in the Great War and had been opposed to the whole bloody business, and how he, a prominent man in his town, a warden in the church too, had been set upon by "a cruel set of imbeciles," as my mother put it, his onetime friends and his rivals, in business and social life, and made to humble himself, forced actually to kiss the flag and swear the oath of allegiance. Remembering,

I felt very close to my uncle and slipped my hand through his arm. "Let's sing while we ride along," I suggested. "We could sing 'Auld Lang Syne,' " said my uncle, "the way we used to. Remember how we all sang when we came to visit you people? Before we took the train?" I squeezed his arm. "Oh, yes," I said. "Good Lord," said my uncle. "You look exactly like your mother!" Then he faced the front and led off; John came in strong, and my uncle leaned forward to look past me at him, nudging me in the ribs to indicate his approval. He had been so delighted with John that he even wanted to meet his parents and proposed stopping off in Michigan for the purpose. John had taken a different view.

"He wants to meet my old man because they are two of a kind. He knows it. Solid types in their hometowns; church members, property owners, that kind of thing." He nodded cynically; he was at war with his father. That might be part of it, but I thought what my uncle really sensed in John was the rascal; he reminded him of his youthful self when, so my mother told me, he had wanted to run off with a showgirl called Gypsy and to team up with her in a vaudeville act. He had rehearsed some catchy songs of the day, among them a number called "Empty Is the Cradle, Baby's Gone."

My mother, not much older than my uncle, had spiked this infatuated fantasy by getting hold of the plot through a secret reading of his letters, going straight to the girl, "a decent sort," who hadn't known he was the last hope of a valiant widowed mother and who nobly ditched him.

My mother had refused to be ashamed about prying into another person's letters. "It's what anyone would do if they cared enough," she had put it. This was one of the last stories she had told me, and hearing it, I was certain that she had probably secretly regaled herself with letters not belonging to her all her life, including letters of mine. When she died, sure enough, I found among her papers a long envelope marked emphatically on the outside: *Private. Don't Open. Destroy.*

How well my mother knew me, I thought. I'm her child, and she knew I'd open it precisely because it says *Destroy.*

It was late at night when I had decided to open the big envelope. My father had gone to bed. We were alone in the big house, the way my mother and father had been before I came home. She would have been sitting up too, long after he had gone to bed. She had always been the last to go to bed, and during the years I lived at home, I would wake from a sound slumber to hear her rustling past my door. "What in the world do you do, sitting up so late?" I had once challenged her. "Heavens, child, it's the only time I get to myself after you've all gone to roost. There's my reading to catch up on, letters to write, and sometimes I just sit and think."

I was sitting at the big dining room table, which had always been cleared after supper for us to do our lessons on and to read at. In the old days my father would be reading a newspaper before he dived into a book; my mother had her book, and each of us four girls had a book, sometimes one that each wanted to read and waited greedily for the other to put down. Then my two older sisters had married; the circle had become more intimate and more to my liking. It seemed to me the strangers had filtered out and left the truly compatible members of the tribe alone. "All they wanted was to get married," I had grumbled. I was in high school when the big girls had left home for little bungalows. "I know," sighed my mother. "It isn't that they didn't marry good boys. But I thought they'd do some traveling, see something of the world. Your uncle offered to send Frances to college. She was such a brilliant student in high school. Both girls had lots of brains. I don't know what happened."

"That Methodist evangelist," I said, "with the curly hair and the Sunbeam Chorus and his big voice, shouting, 'Throw out the lifeline across the dark waves, there is a sinner for someone to save.' "

"Are you sure it went like that?" asked my mother, for she was very particular about language. "Seems to me he thought of himself as the one to do the saving, not 'someone.' "

"Well, they got saved," and I laughed; scornfully, I hoped. "And they got married to men in the church," piped my younger sister, Helen. "And so *finis.*"

We two looked at each other across the table, a long, steady, glowing look; a pact that our lives wouldn't take such a commonplace turn. No, never. Marry? Perhaps. But never as the goal.

"You children don't understand things yet," murmured my mother, disturbed herself. "But don't say *finis*, ever, about anyone. It casts contempt on the role they have chosen, and maybe you don't understand the role or why they chose it." But of course Helen and I thought we did understand, all too well, and as for contempt, yes, we felt that too. It wasn't enough, that's all. Not enough. There was more, infinitely more. The shivering excitement we could get from a book, or from watching the wild geese tear in a long feathery arrow high in the sky, or standing in the shelter of the porch while lightning ripped the black sky, a high wind bending the cottonwoods to swaying wands, or leaning out our bedroom window late at night to sniff the rich, heady odor of wild clover coming in waves from an empty lot next door, told us there was more, much more. Oh, yes, we wanted much more. We wanted everything. Once when a group of girls sat on our front lawn posing questions, one asked, "Do you think it would be better to have loved and lost than never to have loved at all?" Every single one of the girls, with a little squeal, said she would rather never love at all than to love and lose. Except Helen and me. "What?" said one of the girls, tossing a long braid over her shoulder. "You want to suffer?" "No," Helen had said, "but if it has to be." It never crossed our minds, though, that we wouldn't love and be loved. Somewhere—out there—in the world. But we rarely spoke of love; what we talked about incessantly, thought about in the most fanciful varieties, was LIFE. In capital letters. We were in love with life, and what was happening in our daily lives, at home, at school, was only a long apprenticeship.

I had gone back so far that the image of my little sister sitting on the grass was as real as if once more I had been beside her, noting the grass stain on her white dress, and her delicate arms coming out of puffed sleeves. The green stain was like a mark on her; it was like certain tints in her eyes, which could be sea green or grass green, and I appreciated those eyes, for all the rest of the family had gone to seed on blue eyes. Her head, on the stemlike neck, was turned toward me, and yes, we were together in it, and in a way, I had been the leader, she the follower, though when it had come down to real issues, she had always been the bolder. I had a premonition that my mother's envelope would contain some kind of revelation about my sister or about me that I wasn't sure I wanted to see. It was so still in the house and so bare. Most of the family furnishings were already packed away; the old home was going to be broken up for keeps. The sideboard was empty. The oil painting of Mount Hood at sunset executed by my grandmother when she was eighty had been taken down, and out of filial piety, my oldest sister, Frances, meant to give it a home, just as she was going to give a home to my father. I now saw her in an entirely different light than in the early days, when we had been acute rivals without knowing it. I was even grateful for the pricks she had given me; they had taught me how to stand up for myself and how to fight back. Now that she was married and happy, she had become the easy, warm, generous woman she was intended to be and that had simply been locked up in the thin, high-strung girl who had thrown a bottle of ink on the floor the day I was to have a party to celebrate my tenth birthday.

The old black marble clock was still ticking on the mantelpiece in the big living room, which opened through a double door from the dining room where I sat. A few chairs were huddled around a center table, with legs ending in brass claws clutching a glass ball. My bags were packed and stood on the floor, for I was to leave the next day for New York. All of my own problems had been pushed back during the long weeks of my mother's illness and now seemed to be imprisoned among the dresses and shoes, ready to pounce out when the bags would be opened at the end of my journey. I had lighted a fire in the fireplace, for it was the spot in the house my mother had loved. She was proud of it as one of the few real fireplaces in our town; it was like "back East" in her old home. Gas logs she thought obscene, nasty stuff out of a pipe. If you couldn't have a natural fire, better none at all. Above the fireplace was the mantel where we used to put the letters we wrote before going to bed, which my father would pick up on his way to business in the morning. He was an early riser and thought he ought to get to the office by eight o'clock, so often he would have cleared out before we children started on our daily rounds. If there was a letter, it went into his pocket. When my sister and I grew older, and one was away from home, the mantelpiece often boasted a letter to the other. In my memory, she had become my double, and it was my sister I now saw, sitting at the table, pen racing over paper, then sealing the letter, stamping it, putting it on the mantel, calling good night to my mother; then off to bed.

I tore open the envelope, pushing out a bundle of papers written in my mother's beautiful bold hand, some in ink, some in pencil, on the backs of old envelopes or on what appeared to be blank pages torn from the red-lined notebooks Helen and I had kept, in which we stored, as other girls packed lingerie and household linen in a hope chest, those morsels from books that seemed to hold the sacred fire. Or copied out bits of what seemed to us sage observations. Or wrote from the compulsive moment our own strange cries, admonitions, warnings, which through the years had changed from "Beauty is truth, truth beauty" and "To thine own self be true" to a laconic "Never say die" or, mocking the slogans current during the Great War, "Keep a stiff upper lip." There had been lists of books marking the curious deviations, the zigzag path, that led from *Grimms' Fairy Tales* to *Little Women*, from *David Copperfield* and *Vanity Fair* to *Wuthering Heights* and *Madame Bovary*, with sidestepping to *East Lynn*, which a stock company in our Peavy Grand Opera House had resurrected, or to Hall Caine (why had I put down *The Christian* and, rushing from the house, walked blindly for blocks, my senses in a whirl?), and then raced on, with a maddening leap of the pulse, to Chekhov and his Three Sisters pining for Moscow, and on to Turgenev's complex heroines, who, like our aspiring selves, not only believed in the power of love but had daring ideas and ideals, acted rashly but, as we hoped to do, nobly—and, like us, courted life in all its amazing amplitude.

And all those dreamy Russian girls, who strolled away from tea tables on the sunny verandas where butterflies hovered over the empty teacups, to moon under the lime trees, watching the far horizon across the flat steppes—so like our prairies—for the puff of dust that would announce the approaching troika with its ravishing stranger: how *true* they were! How intimately we knew them. Weren't they like us, eager for those rare visits from distant relatives, who would arrive on a magnificent express from which the patrons in the diner would smile knowingly down at our family group, waiting on the platform for the descent of our special messengers from the great world? And no wonder the Three Sisters, when we finally came upon them, haunted us and stiffened our resolve to get beyond helpless yearning to the Real Thing. Or that the very word Moscow became for us the shorthand for a metaphysical state of being; the code for an anticipated New York or Paris where people sitting across from one another at café tables gave way to excited talk and where the very air shimmered with the incandescence of extravagant ideas.

As I had fumbled over the batch of oddly assorted papers, so much had been telescoped to swift scenarios of feeling and action that it was almost a shock to realize that the bold handwriting I was confronting was my mother's hand, charging like the black horses of some Roman charioteer across the arena of what had been the blank pages of our old notebooks. The writing was so alive that for a second it seemed impossible that someone who could write like that should ever die. I fingered through the pages, some of which bore the marks of what my mother had been up to before she sat down to write. One page had a clot of dried paste on it: bread dough. My mother had been "putting the bread to set" before she sat down. The bread would be kneaded, the flour mixed with potato water and yeast, put in a big round tin pan, covered with a clean towel, and stood in a warm place "to rise" during the night. From a compact jumbo mushroom, it would become by morning a mosque-like dome, high above the top of the pan. My mother would knead it again, slap it into round loaves, and stick it in the oven. The loaves would come out a golden brown, would be coated with butter, and placed in the pantry, for the first clean slice "across the loaf " to be spread with homemade apple butter. On another bit of paper, a dull red stain; she must have cut her finger. A thicker splash on a third bit looked like raspberry jam. The little sheaf of papers was a record of my mother's intense night life, for she would be doing a bit of everything: baking bread, cooking jam, which she felt came out best at night, when no one was around to call her away from watching it arrive at the precise second when it had "jelled" and must be snatched from the fire. A book would be left open on the table, and in the early stages of jam making she would have been reading it, her ears tuned to the slow bubbling from the kitchen. Then she would rush to its rescue, and stir, and finally, with the jam in its jars, set to cool, go back to the table again. There was a needle run through the corner of one paper, threaded with a lingering bit of violet-colored silk. Those needles! For she had made all our dresses and with such style. Probably she had been making a blouse to send to me, the daughter away from home, when she absentmindedly stuck that needle in the paper. I knew I was regaling myself with these intimate signs to postpone reading the papers. Was it right for me to look? She had said *Destroy*, but hadn't that been intended for my father, in case the papers fell into his hands, not for me?

She had always been protective of my father's peace of mind. I could remember how she would ignore the sound of the four girls busy at some petty bickering among ourselves until that moment when a glance at the clock told her it was time for my father to arrive home. Then she would come to the doorway and stand firm: "Now I want you girls to quiet down. It's time for Papa to come home, and I don't want him to find the house in a turmoil. He works for us all day and deserves peace and quiet." We piped down at once. But he had been left out, too, of the conferences, the hesitations, the exciting debates that concerned the important decisions of our lives. He had been out of it, in his curious male fashion; our prop and provider must have been a lonely man.

But on our Sunday walks, or on picnics at Riverside Park by the Big Sioux River, where the tablecloth had spread itself like a white domino on the grass and the five females had planted their finery of dainty muslin beside the reclining graceful aloof figure of the one male we could boast of, his form and his presence had always proclaimed him the almost invisible center, the hub to our wheel, the substance that allowed our fanciful venturing to take flight. Without him, what were we? Even as small children, when we still had the notion that the doctor brought the new baby, it was clear that without him, no doctor would come. And I could remember that my first intimation of the delight grownups shared with one another had come one early summer morning, when the bright light made it seem time to get out of bed, and I had come upon the breakfast table, where my father and mother were sitting, quietly talking, holding hands, and how surprised they were to see me. I went outdoors into grass heavy with dew. The road was a deep plush of shadowed dust, and the neighborhood cows were moving in a soft mooing group, like so many school-girls, to their pasture at the edge of town. Our cow had raced down to join the sisterhood, her brass bell coyly tin-kling, and my father had come out of the house, bareheaded, beside my mother, holding his face up to drink in the joyful sun. Then he had gone off to be swallowed up in the myste-rious abyss of business for a long day.

But there were times, perhaps when the circus had come to town, when we tracked him down in the cool of the big warehouse, surrounded by the huge threshers and plows. Behind, in the gloom, near the waiting dainty sur-reys and phaetons, which nobody seemed ever to buy, our father would be chatting with huge red-faced farmers, whose legs in funnels of blue denim were as solid as the pistons of the big trains. He then looked delicate and shy; his voice, too, made him a stranger among strangers. They said words differently—pronounced coffee as cawfee—and chewed tobacco, cutting the plug with heavy-handled knives. A spittoon in my father's office honored their tastes; my father smoked a pipe or cigars.

It had been a bid to self-importance when I was called upon to "keep office" for my father on those days when a big shipment of farm machinery to nearby towns kept him on the go. To answer the phone, to take down long-distance calls, jotting down the names of parts required for repairs, which might then demand as many as forty tags for ship-ment, addressed in my own round, gawky hand; to be intro-duced to the farmers. "This is my office boy," and to stand erect shaking hands with a paw that made my fingers melt like a marshmallow—all this was marvelous, a taste of the bustling world outside. It was much better than the kitchen, which, in spite of its delicious smells, could be a trap. If you didn't watch your step, you'd be in a little bungalow, beating eggs for keeps. Dusting and sweeping was a different business; my mother, a wonderful cook and a skillful maker of clothes, was careless of threads on the floor, dust on the grand piano. Didn't she realize how beautiful it could look when the dining table was shined to a gloss, the keys of the piano were washed to a glistening white and ebony, the leaves of the umbrella plant sprayed to a shiny green? I could tackle these jobs with an appalling sense of virtue and then sit back to gloat on the effect. It might have been a preview of the interiors painted by the great Dutch masters that, at a later date, were to entrance me. Nor did I mind that I made a nuisance of myself in my devotion to order and beauty. My mother had only to leave the house on a shopping trip before I leaped for the carpet sweeper, rushing it over the Brussels carpet, where the roses bloomed in big patches of yellow and red. Guilty, hurrying, I would be flicking the duster as I heard the door open and rushed to hide the evidence. But my mother couldn't be fooled. Coming in with her hands full, she would drop her parcels, stand poised, sniffing, say reproachfully, "Josie, you've been raising the dust again."

But those powerful farmers, their mouths stained at the corners with the brown of tobacco juice, their big thumbs hooked into the straps of faded overalls, had been our nemesis as nature had been their albatross. Three seasons of bad luck had canceled out years of labor. The sun burned up the corn; a half hour of hail slaughtered the crop that was to pay the interest due on their mortgaged farms, also what was alas due my father. My father had stepped down from his status as "an independent businessman." The business was changing fast, but in his day-to-day absorption he had not noticed. "I must have been asleep at the switch," he would mutter in the empty weeks to follow, when he seemed so out of place, staying at home.

My mother refused to admit he wouldn't eventually be "independent" once again, in a business of his own. She was in a ferment of ways to help out; if she could only think of some invention! "The silliest things are invented," she insisted. "No one sees what they may be, until they arrive. Everything we take for granted had its beginnings in someone's brains." Then she puzzled and made a small invention of her own. It was the days before steel-wool pads were used for cleaning pots. Cleaning pots was a chore that could be made easier. There should be something that would not scratch a good pot, so it couldn't be a blade. A small piece of wood, like a spade, could be the thing. She took her idea to a carpenter, who made her one exactly right. Tried on a pot that had been allowed to burn its contents, it was certainly remarkable! She had two dozen made, and each one was stamped with a printed slogan: "Gem Scraper." Our groceryman agreed to display her wares; none sold. Doubtless she had envisioned a small fortune, busy housewives smilingly manipulating her Gem over irascible pots and pans. But there was no advertising campaign. They would have to be taught, as the alphabet is taught. Who was to teach them? Ideas swirled in her head, and were still agitating her when my father got back on his feet. He would not be independent but, as my mother delicately put it, be working for "another business firm." If he was no longer *out,* he was certainly several steps *down.* He could support my mother and himself but hardly undertake to back me or my sister in our plans for education. We were out in the world, pitched out, but it was not the one we had looked for. I had three years at college; my sister had graduated from high school with honors. We were as smart as whips, though, as my father was fond of saying, and where there was a will, there was a way. Our parents, who could give us no money, had by invisible means and through indirection given us a wealth of self-confidence. We had never heard them lament that they had no sons.

When I was still a small child, my mother had pushed my bangs back from my forehead and, looking down at me intently, had murmured, "I wonder what you'll be. A lawyer, perhaps?" thus flattering my budding argumentative powers. Even in our modest town we had women who set an example for a girl ambitious to go beyond the domestic circle. Our family doctor was married to a woman who was also a practicing physician. At the Unitarian church, which the four girls had attended until our older sisters fell under the spell of a Methodist evangelist, there were two women preachers, who wore long dresses falling in beautiful sculptured folds of a soft material called nun's veiling. Miss Spender was a sibyl in gray; Mrs. Howe, whose husband was an author, wore black. Their voices very low, musical, and vaguely inspiring. One did not need to comprehend what they said; they represented something, just by standing in a pulpit and exercising their powers as spiritual guides. After the Unitarians, the Methodist minister was a shock; a huge, untidy man with the contour of a Samuel Johnson. Where the Unitarians had been cool, the Methodists were hot. The Unitarians had been genteel; on Easter, big baskets of colored eggs adorned the pulpit and were distributed to each Sunday school pupil after the services. The Methodists went in for Easter lilies; little girls in white, with corkscrew curls, sang in a chirping choir under the rostrum. The Methodists could be rank, noisy, and, calling each other "brother" and "sister," would race down the aisle after church to fall upon one another's necks with the fervor of long-lost relatives. They fascinated, repelled, and aroused me to a curiosity that blanked out the gentle voice of the teacher of our class, a smart young woman in a beautiful pleated skirt with a transparent blouse revealing the ravishment of an embroidered "corset cover" threaded with pink ribbons.

A score of other classes going on simultaneously in the church auditorium offered gaudy divertissement. Sun trickled playfully through the stained-glass windows to quilt comical patches of blue and red on the grizzled head and nose of the elderly leader of the Adult Bible Class, Brother Small, as he wrestled for the soul of the heretic, the bandy-legged colonel, who, a glutton for argument, chewed away at his doubts of the existence of God with the fervor of a drunkard. The members of the church took pride in their unrepentant sinner, who compelled them to exercise the sinews of their belief. As for the colonel, he gloated at his impersonation of Lucifer, positively reeling up the aisle at the conclusion of the class, aglow with the fever of the combat. The booming and shouting from the elders' corner could eclipse the attractions going on elsewhere: young people flirting above the top of lesson papers, or giggling in corners, thrilling to the meeting of male and female fingers as they clasped the shared hymnbook. The little Sunday school lesson leaflets might cut the Bible down to grammar school tedium, but there were members of the congregation whose expressions, as they sang "Abide with Me," were as exalted as the saints'.

At the Unitarian church there had been a wonderful storyteller, a placid woman in a little bonnet covered with plush pansies, who could bring to life the story of Joseph and his coat, Ruth and her sheaves of wheat. Mrs. Groniger had made the Bible people live, breathe, and sweat. I could see Absalom hanged by his long hair from the tree and his father eating his heart out, as he sat in sackcloth and ashes. Back home I had to repeat these stories to my mother, and I can see myself when my head barely came to the top of the kitchen table. My mother would be preparing a big steak for our Sunday dinner, but she would pay attention to every word, encouraging me to add further details and rewarding me by cutting off a bit of the raw meat to drop into my mouth, held open like a little bird's. Laughing and joking with my mother, the Bible people did not seem very different from our neighbors. Hadn't a next-door neighbor, an old woman with shriveled yellow skin, wailed one night in a high, piercing lament that made us all shiver as we sat at the table at suppertime and looked at one another with awe? "Poor creature," my father had said.

"But what's wrong with her?"

My father cleared his throat and looked at my mother. Then he said, "It's in the paper. They must have just now told her. Her son was hanged for murder in Utah." And for the next hour we could hear the awesome sound. That noise was grief, the voice of David mourning. It had swelled into some monstrous clot outside our door: dark, dense, and lonely, trying to break in.

With the Unitarians, it had been the Old Testament. The Methodists favored the New Testament. At revival meetings, where I was a curious spectator, I studied the penitents, wondering what sins had soiled their souls that needed to be washed in the blood of the lamb. Old ladies who wouldn't hurt a fly, young girls who were as meek as oysters, rose to their feet to testify that their sins had been washed whiter than snow; Jesus loved them, and now they were happy every day. Sin was undoubtedly dark, mysterious, and frightfully attractive. There was an odd monotony about the testimonials that sometimes made me twitch with an internal nervous laughter. I would be frantic for fear of suddenly tittering aloud, and covering my mouth with a handkerchief, I would try to turn the convulsive impulse into a harsh barking cough. My little sister would pluck at my elbow. "What's wrong with you?" And I might wonder myself, feel chagrined and half conscious that I was concealing a hidden envy for some mystery I could not fathom. Detached, curious, wondering, my sister and I would sit sedately when the invitation to the mourners' bench gradually emptied the pews around us, leaving us high and dry as the conspicuous unrepentants. We would actually have liked to join the throng moving toward the altar, but couldn't. When old ladies bent tenderly above us, asking in yearning voices, "Don't you want to give your hearts to Jesus? Don't you want to be saved?" we felt so embarrassed that we could not even shake our heads but stared straight ahead, stonily, waiting for them to give us up and go away.

My older sisters had been "saved," and their state was conspicuous in our household. We younger ones looked hard at them to see in what way they had undergone some miraculous transformation. What transformation they brought seemed to bring discomfort for the rest of us. They nagged my mother about my father's condition on earth, which imperiled his situation in heaven. He was not "saved." My mother was impatient with them and answered that they might search the wide world over and not find a more honorable man. The big girls sobbed that being honorable and morally good was not sufficient; he had to be born again and washed in lamb's blood. For a brief period they were tiresomely pious, attending four different services on

Sunday and several during the week. They disapproved of everything "worldly"; censored my father for playing cards on the night of his lodge meeting and for going to baseball games on Sunday, a cigar in his mouth and wearing a new jaunty straw hat. Dancing and the theater were *out;* even taking a streetcar ride on Sunday to get the cooling breezes was frowned upon. "What a trial," my mother sighed, and my father, looking up philosophically from his paper, consoled, "Don't fret yourself. They'll either take to a hairshirt or ease up. It's too strict to last."

In time the church itself eased up, but long before that their religion did not prevent my sisters and their friends from bubbling with an effervescent sociality that was wonderfully diverting. Their gang of long-legged young men in starched collars and girls in fluffy dresses would group around our piano to bang out "When the harvest moon is shining on the river" or "I'll go chicken stealing for you," with a variety of arch and flirtatious exchanges that made their performance better fun than the schoolbooks my sister and I were presumed to be studying in the adjoining room. Staring out at the performers with the detached amused expressions of customers in the best theater seats expecting good entertainment and the privilege of criticism, we enraged the older girls, who stormed that they couldn't enjoy themselves with "those two owls forever ogling" us. My sister and I might nudge one another to whisper, "Aren't they silly?" but the scene in the parlor charmed the senses even as we rejected it as nothing like the "real life" awaiting us.

In my memory I can see the scene as if it had been a painting, the figures frozen in angelic attitudes, the colors brought to a burning intensity. The girls' white dresses become frosty bloom above the red and yellow flowers in the carpet; the crisp lace curtains at the window, patterned with friezes of embroidered flowers and grasses, show a ghosty resemblance to old tapestry. Now the stiff high collars of the young man would be odd period pieces. But as the music plays, the glossy heads sway, the mouths round, as they gently nod to one another across the top of the accompanist's stack of honey-colored hair.

If I see it so vividly now, it is because I saw it then, greedily drinking in every detail at the same time that I was compelled to mock or never go beyond the border of that pictorial frame. The pleasures of mocking and criticizing were enormous. My sister and I could take off Mrs. Gregg and Mrs. Orr, mother and daughter, who appeared to our youthful eyes of an identical age and who lived in two great houses, side by side, on our block. Rich, deserted, both of them, by their husbands, stingy, reported never able to keep a servant longer than two weeks, they consoled themselves in the cool of a summer evening by sitting side by side on a little iron bench, munching hard candies while their hired man watered the expanse of vast lawns. Or I might enliven Sunday dinner by reporting to my father, "There's a kissing bell at Sunday school. When the superintendent taps it after church for Sunday school to begin, all the ladies buzz around, kissing one another. The bell says, time for kissing." My older sisters burned with indignation. "How can she lie like that?" and when my father rewarded me with a burst of chuckles, they turned on him. "You shouldn't encourage her to lie, you shouldn't." But I stuck to my story. It was true that Brother Weidel tapped a bell. It was true that the sisters went around embracing one another.

The church provided a weekly stipend of drama, and it wasn't religion that took me there every Sunday. If the faithful were not spared humiliations—the wife of a devout parishioner ran off with a flashy drummer—there were old people as steady as church steeples, whom I was later to identify with the Old Believers in Russian novels; gentle souls who could walk up the church aisle after a sermon, their faces alight with the inspiration of the prophets, and, in a dreamy trance, appear to float down rather than descend the staircase, calling out singsong greetings, or benevolently tap a child on the head; and it was true, they seemed to exude a kind of generous love that was as real as their stubby shoes or the white crowns of their heads. I had an enormous respect for their enthralled visions. Didn't they look the way I felt when, in my dreams, I stood lightly poised, arms lifted slowly as a bird's wings to soar from the ground above the tops of trees, over the roofs of houses, and even to pass over wide rivers? My bones felt more than my head knew. In dreams I was one of the saints or one of the demons. It hardly mattered. Both were extraordinary.

The extraordinary! Only the extraordinary was worthwhile. And the weather, the overpowering head in summer, the piercing cold of winter, invited dreams. Sunk in the cushions of a green chair in a darkened room, with windows tightly closed to shut out the blazing sun, I passed the summer in a trance. If interrupted from a book, I would raise a blank expression and, swollen with the intoxication of visions, recognize reluctantly my mother's command to come to shell the peas. Peas, what were peas? And her added "I know you don't want to, but do it anyhow" lifted the burden of moral guilt. I didn't need to pretend to be a mother's eager helper; I could get it over with fast, and like a sleepwalker return to the delirium of the Other World. The intimations of that world were multiple; they were like weeds that flowered, turned to pods, and burst with scattering seed. The insights of one summer could look ridiculous the next; doors slammed, windows opened to other views, and the long hoot of the train as it passed Dyckman's crossing flashed a signal to the future. A woman who took a trip to nearby Le Mars figured in the society notes. A businessman journeying to Des Moines acquired luster. The family who summered at Lake Okoboji became people of distinction. Families clustered on their front porches, and in the long after-dark of a hot summer evening, the light dresses of the women and girls glimmered like great moths. The ladder of a man's suspenders climbed a chaste white shirt.

Our town might be a prairie wildflower, deserted by the major railroads for more flashy Omaha, but we had an opera house called the Peavy Grand, a relic of the now deflated boom days, equipped with gilded boxes, bloated cherubs floating above the proscenium, and a spangled curtain. Once the immortal Joe Jefferson had played Rip Van Winkle to a full house, but I had never gone beyond a spectacular performance of *Ben-Hur*, with live horses, harnessed to gold chariots, thundering across the stage, driven by young men in flaring skirts with fillets of ribbon around their heads. Or in the early days, an Uncle Tom show, where the big excitement was little Eva going to heaven on a squeaky cloud. The hounds to chase Eliza might be conscripted from local talent. One of them, recognizing a young master in the audience, could come to a dead stop, tail wagging, tongue lolling over the footlights, while his desperate owner hissed, "Sic 'em, Rover, sic 'em," as Eliza pranced across the hunks of simulated ice. But the glitter of the chandeliers, the smells fuming up from the carpet and from peanuts, were intoxicating. The orchestra manfully tootling away, the starched shirts of the musicians, the rustle of programs, were the authentic shadows of the Real Thing to be revealed one fine day.

The magicians changed faces and costumes; were invisible as the wind, hid in the lilac bush, whispered from the willow. Or beckoned to the high yellow bluffs hanging over the Missouri, where the pasqueflowers with their gray fur stalks lifted pale lavender cups with burning yellow inner crowns. Or the magicians might hold aloft a torch of wild plum blossom at the edge of a dry run, or spurt patches of juicy violets among the cinders of the railroad tracks. Autumn brought the magicians out in full cry. The hills rang with bluebells, and the wild sumac rained its red lava down. From the high bluffs the Big Sioux looked no more than a thin thread of mercury slithering into the cobra jaws of the mighty Missouri. Or our invisible ones might entice us to let our canoe enter the swift current of the Big Sioux as it headed for the mouth of the Missouri, when, caught in an eddy, on our knees, we stroked for our very lives, in a sweat of energy and fear, until we inched back, out of the valley of death, out of the jaws of hell. Oh, gallant six hundred! Scared, exultant, laughing idiotically once we were safe, we knew better than to boast of our exploit to parents who trusted our common sense. It was our secret. We knew everything and nothing.

Was Rosa Bonheur's *Horse Fair* on the wall of the school stairway the last word in painting? What was Louisa Alcott once you had discovered the stormy mad Brontë sisters on their bleak moor, or the enigmatic George Sand, who smoked cigars and lived openly with one or another celebrated lover? As the local wits deprecated the East and the ogres of Wall Street out of envy, we downgraded the Midwest out of longing. Nourished by the juice of its grasses, incited by the enormous blue flag of its skies, wiser in the blood than we knew, we were ignorant as toads of the way the world ran. So, it seemed, were our elders, when in 1914 news of the war in Europe found them stunned and wanting.

Who had dreamed of war? When Teddy Roosevelt was President, a sirloin steak could be had for twenty cents. Taft upped the price, but milk remained steady at five cents a quart. Mothers on our block continued to keep young daughters hard at piano practicing, and painful strains of a "Please Do Waltz" or a limping "Moonlight" Sonata greeted the dusk. Doped by oyster suppers, blandished by ice cream socials under swaying Chinese lanterns on the church lawn, boys limbered up for the future by shaving a neighbor's grass for a dime. Girls stitched away at pillow-cases heavy with embroidered daisy chains for a hope chest doomed to yellow unless the bridegroom cometh.

For my parents, youth was mysterious and allowed to be so. Neither one of them required a manual to understand their young, or to leave us alone, or to mismanage us and thwart us, sometimes for better as for worse. Neither parent took us aside to tell us about the birds and the bees. A set of encyclopedias, the daily paper, the shady doings of Becky Sharp, the tactics of Jane Eyre with the tumultuous husband of a mad wife, the eyes in our heads, and the senses in our bodies were presumed to be sufficient guides unto the day. Our parents were no prudes. All that glittered was not gold, and the stiff shirtfront of a church deacon might hide a lustful heart. The tightwad was gold's harlot, and he who pinched pennies sucked a sore paw. My mother was old-fashioned. When people died she said they were dead, not that they had passed away. Of an idle Sunday we might pore over the yellowed journals of her father, who, reporting the death of his own father, mingled tenderness with the forthright, commenting: "It was a hot day in July. He died of a Sunday. If we had not had ice we could not have kept him." Or we might stumble across a batch of old family letters and find one from this same grandfather's much older cousin, Solomon, who had counseled my grandfather, bereaved by the death of two infants from scarlet fever, " 'Tis fearful to lose a child. But take comfort. Thee is young and can make more. Alas, for me my time is past. All is over except the pangs and pains." If not weaned on painful circumstances, my parents had been inducted into the mysteries of unwanted disasters, the uneven distributions in the affairs of life, fortune and favor, long before they joined their separate destinies. My identity was dyed by my mother's fables. A Gehenna lurked in every bloodstream. Even the bedtime songs my father liked to sing carried the stain of wild blackberry sadness from a wayside past well behind him: "Oh, Father Grimes, that dear old soul, we ne'er shall see no more." Or we might puzzle over a long ballad sung without punctuation, and beginning, "I was born in New Jersey one morning last summer I got a dispatch that my uncle was dead." As the follow-up indicated a train ride, a romantic widow, and a stolen watch, all beyond the capacity of a baby born last summer, I complained to my father, who, irritated at the interruption, braved a comma. He was all for this world and the Now. His own past had withered away with his marriage; he seldom wrote a letter.

Marriage had stimulated my mother's appetite for her heritage and linked her with her brothers, to the east and to the west, and with a last lone sister, married to a grocer in Oregon who, like a lily of the field, left the shop to his wife's ministrations while he sat by a brook, wearing a natty beard and a straw hat, painting pictures of shadows on the long grass. Our attic was larded with four swaying sacks of family letters, journals, account books, and worthless deeds belonging to generations going back to Christian Frey, who had immigrated from Zurich to Pennsylvania around 1700, had acquired a great tract of land, married a Veronica Rhodes, the daughter of an English judge in Allentown, and begat eleven children, all of whom died before he did. The heads of families had staked their claim to perpetuity in records of births, marriages, and deaths. Infants perished of croup, summer sickness, and "thrush" (probably diphtheria), or, dying stillborn, were given long names and noted in the record. A Joshua and a Joseph appeared in every generation; Aaron and Daniel came in strong. They married Maria Annas and Catherines, or a Nancy or Hortensia, and begat quantities of children, whose dates of death were sometimes solemnized in a prayer book beside a favorite verse. The pages of Gray's "Elegy in a Country Churchyard" were bedewed with the stains of a faded violet, the petal of a red poppy. A trigonometry was punctuated with ghosty blades of meadow grass. My sister and I liked to refer to the sacks of family loot hanging from the attic rafters as the four headless horsemen, and on a stormy night of a high wind, as we sat in the cozy living room below, the groaning from their gallows could chill the blood; we fancied we could heard an anguished sighing, the murmured complaints of bones shorn of hope.

The male line of my mother's family had not always been sheet anchors to the wind. Her own father, Joshua Frey, had died suddenly, leaving a young widow with six children, one a babe in arms. He had just returned from a laborious trip overland to Wisconsin, where he had gone to find a good location for a company of Swiss immigrants coming up by riverboat from New Orleans. He seems to have been a man who could do almost anything. He was a surveyor of roads and land, and, in spite of a scientific turn of mind, a "finder" of water, with a willow branch. He was a scrivener, who wrote letters and legal papers in English for many of his neighbors, who often could speak and write only in German. Inheriting land, he speculated in more land and got in pretty deep, for when he died he had nothing much for his widow after his debts were squared. But neither his widow nor his children ever spoke of him except as an exceptional man and a "noble work." He had gone to the state legislature, and perhaps for some battles on the floor of the House, which I never got the hang of, he was presumed to "have suffered for the Right," like a character out of the pages of Gogol. For some reason I never took to him and preferred his black-sheep wastrel brother, Jacob, whose affairs my grandfather accounted for in a censorious diary, claiming that he had been an unrepentant drunkard who, dying of cancer of the tongue, refused the visits of the local preacher and "poured the wine down his throat as long as he could swallow." My grandmother was left with no fortune except her children. A rich brother-in-law, Uncle Blank of Bethlehem, might have come to the rescue but came forward with no more than the wherewithal to buy the widow a grudging sewing machine. She took her brood to Philadelphia and launched herself as a seamstress, setting herself up in a workroom employing girls, where my mother at the age of eleven busily pedaled away each day after school.

Passionate for the education she was not to get—it was all to go to her brothers—my mother seemed to have picked up her cultivated tastes from the very air. Or those becoming graces had been magnetized to her over mystifying airways that often paralleled the lines of love. A fat volume of Shakespeare's plays, including the sonnets, had come from the mysterious Mrs. Farrell, an actress friend of her older brother, who had read the plays aloud to the young girl in what my mother described as "a thrilling voice" and whose intimate connection with the family was only revealed to her years later, when she discovered her friend to have been her brother's mistress—the dark woman of the sonnets, as she put it—who had died giving birth to his child. Another item, a volume of the works of Oliver Goldsmith in lavender and gold, had been the gift of John Gason, a young Englishman whom she had met in Philadelphia and with whom she had fallen so deeply in love that she waited seven years for him to return from England or to send for her. It had happened during one of those bleak interludes when her brothers, always ready to lift the family up to opulence, had cast them down. My mother had studied telegraphy as a way to earn a living, and when she sometimes tapped out the Morse code for "I love you" on the breadboard for the edification of her children, I liked to imagine that she was secretly remembering the elusive lover of her youth.

But it had been my father, a real man, not an elegant tintype, who had rescued her from the phantasmagoria of idle dreams. If the lore of my mother's family—her roving brothers, their reckless venturing, their passionate doomed love affairs—was our first oral library, the revelations never issued as tedious chronological history. A bustling event, or the way the grocer boy whistled as he slammed the goods on the kitchen table, could be the bait to fetch to the surface some shining trout of memory. Or a cloud in the sky, a ripple in the grass, summoned the flute that a brother had played in the family trio, where my mother had presided at the piano and a sister hugged a violin. Or her own approaching death called back the image of her mother, sitting in her workroom so long ago, with the sewing machines covered for Sunday, looking up to sigh, "Here I sit, on a dry twig, piping notes of sorrow."

Life oozed into literature and back again with augmented powers. For my sister and me, true literature, as we put it, was not about life. It *was* life, as authentic as bread and salt, an essence that passed into your blood and filled your lungs with the air you breathed. It was the differentiating power, to separate this from that and to shake you out of the notion that the straight and narrow was the only way. Many paths invited, looped the loop, twisted into tunnels and out again into meadows, or twitched through high grass above a murmuring sea. We *had* to believe the choice could be yours. The risk was all. If we thought of it as a kind of celestial handball, it was well we did. We needed to be exalted, lest we help ourselves to nothing. Without any conscious intent, my mother had unveiled the male figure—to be so important in our lives— as wholly paradoxical: certain at one time or another to herald stormy misfortune, even disaster, but without whom life could offer no more than a tepid drama. So inextricably had she mingled her fate with that of the menfolk of her family that her first thought was in defense of my father when he had to step down a peg, warning us, "He's got brains. But not the right sort. He's too honest." Or, "What we need is a little capital," thus conjuring up that panacea for human ills, which cast so long a shadow. Her invocation to "capital" was so personalized that it had for me the appearance of an allegorical form, resembling the replica of the Victory of Samothrace at the head of the stairs in our high school, where the great wings spread ominously as we mounted upward.

•   •   •

When my father's business collapsed, I was not yet twenty; my sister, seventeen. Stuffed with romantic notions, gulled by books, we preened our feathers and prepared to conquer. But what on earth could we do? Young females might pound a typewriter and learn shorthand, or teach. The first we did not know; for the second we were unprepared. I imagined that because I had finished my third year at the University of Iowa I might qualify as a refined teacher of English literature in some high school. When a covey of letters, praising myself, brought no response, I fell back on a teachers' agency in Des Moines, where for the sum of a month's salary they pulled out a plum: teacher of the seventh and eighth grades at fifty-five dollars per month. The town was stranded in the dry belt, had no river, and was mis-named Stratford. With less schooling to her credit, my sister had no trouble getting a country school where in one big room she would handle eight grades of husky farm kids. Her school was in the corn belt, three miles from a small town called Correctville.

Neither of us had any intention of making teaching a life's work. Our goal was not to educate others but to get more knowledge for ourselves. It was a day when scholarships for bright students were not to be had for the asking. If we knew anything, it was that we would be expected to help ourselves or succumb. If we accepted the inevitable and busied ourselves with details, it seemed to promise compensations. No matter how it turned out, we would be gaining "experience," and in the hot rush of youth, any experience, good or bad, was better than tepid time serving. How I valued experience, that great sage! Of the true education—sexual understanding and charitable feelings for others—I knew next to nothing. Feeling myself an ignorant vessel, I had prowled, early in the game, among the shelves of the stackroom of our public library without fishing up anything more illuminating than *What Every Boy Should Know*. Hampered by an excess of self-sufficiency and a reluctance to admit that I was ignorant, I never thought to ask a few simple questions. Itching with curiosity, troubled with inexplicable rashes of bad temper, plagued by dreamy broodings, which seemed to put a heavy pane of glass between me and others, I had stared at my image in the mirror on my sixteenth birthday, and seeing a pale, intense face with huge eyes, mounted by a mop of unruly fair hair under a hideous green felt hat, I had sneered, "So *this* is sweet sixteen!"

But a new librarian, swishing in copper-colored silk, a goddess from New York City, had transformed our stuffy reading rooms into bowls of light, with ferns at the window. Even *Poole's Index* was redeemed from its dark corner. Her invitation to ask for any book I might want, which, if not in stock, she would promptly order, offered a dazzling prospect. Primed with a review in a magazine of a work called *The Sexual Question*, by Forel, I made bold to ask for it. It was ordered and handed across the counter as casually as a cookbook. Though it might have been a handy guide to the Berlin I was to encounter years later, it was a witches' sabbath for present uses. I could hardly believe the human skin could contain so many diabolical juices. Reading it, I felt of the elect and, in the know, was further encouraged to look down my nose at less informed contemporaries, mere chits ogling schoolboys.

Schoolboys, too, were beneath me, hardly able to measure up to my romantic notions. They were literally smaller, for I had shot up unreasonably after a long siege of scarlet fever when I was twelve. Kept out of school for half a year, I was chagrined on entering high school to find I towered above most of my male contemporaries. When an accidental touch of a handsome boy with a beautiful voice set up an inner palsy, I disdained my feelings and avoided encounters. Pouring energy into a militant pursuit of knowledge, I was at ease with boys only on debating teams or sitting in conferences about our school paper. I had no small talk. I was engaged in inner colloquies, and though it is said that the young never imagine they can die, for months at a time I secretly brooded upon death. Illness can unhinge the door to eternity; mine flapped to every changing breath. When I was three I had nearly perished from diphtheria; then, at a later date, scarlet fever. Though my mother consoled me with the notion that I must be intended for something special, as I had survived so much, I felt death as a trap, which could be sprung at any moment.

The dread of death told me I had a body; fear of mortality became a secret shame. In my bedroom, with the door shut, I would sit on the bed, no longer able to find pleasure in what now seemed trivial handiwork. For I had transformed the plain pine furniture with layers of white enamel paint, as prescribed by the *Ladies' Home Journal;* the walls were sprigged with a fanciful flowered paper, giving me the illusion of a bower. My mother, proud of my endeavors, had bought a new rug of a heavenly blue color, to lie on the matting before my bed. The window looked out on a big meadow where vacant lots expanded in a burst of tall red clover, buzzing with bees and sunlight. A framed motto on the wall, a present from my mother, told me:

> And so I find it well to come
> For deeper rest to this still room,
> For here the habit of the soul
> Feels less the outer world's control
> And by this silence, multiplied

By these still forms on every side,
The world that time and sense hath known
Falls off, and leaves us God alone.

There had been earlier moments when to come into my
room, to read the lines of this motto, had stirred me with
lofty premonitions. Now the words turned to insipid verbi-
age or even worse—glum foreboding. I had no wish to be
with God alone, not even with my mother's God, who was
already everywhere—in the grass, a bird's song, the cloud
in the sky, and the voice that said "Good night." With a
finger pressed hard on the blue vein of my pulse, I would
take the count. It was frightfully slow, a deep, ponderous
throb. It was always to be slow, and years later, Ernest
Hemingway was to tell me that a steady slow pulse was the
mark of a good prizefighter; he cited one notable who had
fought three dozen rounds. But at twelve I had no such
assurance; I fancied myself doomed. Then I forgot the pulse
and, with a throat ravaged by scarlet fever, dreamed of
tasting blood. Feverishly poring over the pages of our
household guide, *Dr. Pierce's Golden Medical Discoveries*, I
traced the symptoms of tuberculosis. Hadn't my father's
two sisters died within a week of each other of galloping
consumption? Convicted of fever, trapped with the infamy
of death, I wrapped myself in a straitjacket of sheets to await
each night the telltale sweat. Above me, the floorboards of
the attic throbbed; the night poured its dews through an
open window. The cottonwoods sighed a dirge to my
shroud. Alone, I died, over and over, and in a blind panic.
Lofty lines from literature vanished in the smoke of despair;
my little sister sleeping beside me was not even a consoling
stone.

Restless with symptoms, I agitated the pages of *Dr.*

Pierce, rummaging for clues. Why was I always running to the bathroom just before a timid escort arrived to accompany me to what should have been a jolly party? Why did my face turn to burning fire? Why couldn't I be pale, composed, crack witty jokes? I must have Bright's disease or be fated for it. When I overheard an adult comment that marshmallows were good for the kidneys, I bought a sackful every day, and like a cannibal chewed on frenzied health as I walked the two miles home from high school. Life was sweet. Its rags and its tatters, priceless. The kiss of death ravished me for living at any price; I would have chosen to be a one-legged, one-eyed beggar rather than nothing at all.

My body was speaking a language I was too ignorant to interpret; to its murmurings I turned a deaf ear, or I translated its messages to elevated thoughts, where they swam like Cypriot fish in the sky of my aspirations. I had been inducted into womanhood early; I was only eleven when the sign came. My mother had taken me to a room apart and, closing the door, spoken tenderly of the mysteries of the womb. "Didn't you ever notice anything? Your older sisters?" But my thoughts had been either in the ether or puzzling with language, wondering what was meant by a line in our newspaper that read: "Mabel Butler's resort on Pearl Street was raided last evening. . . ." Nor to my question "What's a resort?" had my mother's answer, "A watering place," been satisfactory. "But where is there a watering place on Pearl Street?" I demanded. And my badgered mother, reluctant to let in the stink of the underworld, lamely answered, "Well, it's a kind of gaming place too," which had been correct enough, though I couldn't know why.

Now we were trapped in a room together, mother and daughter. Savaged by the inequalities of her wisdom, my ignorance, we eyed one another, each dreading to speak. She tiptoed delicately but firmly. The spell would be cast upon me for from three days to five every single month. Until death do us part? was in my thoughts. Or when? I couldn't bring myself to ask. "Be a little careful those days, don't go jumping around—you always leap from high places like a squirrel. Keep your feet dry." But from what depths did a shiver convulse her face with its shadow? Why was she so austere, so pale, so meltingly tender? "You're early for this. Fourteen is the commoner age. But then you got your first tooth sooner than most," and she brightened, seeing hopeful signs of a precocious artfulness. Then she was telling me that this was the first signal of the body's ripening: for love, for children. But indignant, she added, "But you're only a child yourself. It's too soon." Her news had subdued and astonished me. I was boiling with questions to which I could not, for the life of me, have given tongue. I stalked away from her, rigid with self-important dignity, seething with wonderment, dread, anticipation of I hardly knew what.

Dr. Pierce, though verbose on the subject of catarrh, could not enlighten me. I sought news in the public library, mousily prowling the shelves, sniffing here and there after the lines of life, which filmed out to a design in constant flux. The girl was barely an adolescent, when she became a woman; through the magic of love, she was a mother; but an inexorable flood tide carried her beyond childbearing; she shoaled on a reef called "the change of life." It was too much and not enough. Not enough by any means. What was I to make of it all? For the moment I made nothing at all. I was amazed to discover myself of a vast company, exclusively female, who were regularly reminded in language of the blood of what they were. Not only my mother, my sisters, my teachers, but the Brontë girls, George Sand! The Queen of England! Was it a thistle or a rose? I could not say. I must grow and grope. A mysterious something lived within my bark. It had lived in Dido, who had cast herself upon the flames when Aeneas put out to sea. Had she died of it? A power stronger than the fear of death was awesome. The sign had come that the power was in me, and waiting.

My body had spoken its first piece, but what had it said? I would have to bide my time and wait. It seemed that I was no longer on the sunny bank of the river, sporting with mere children. I had passed over to the shady, grownup side. Called upon to take my place among a throng, who would I be? I ransacked the cupboard of my mind for clues, but the shelves were suddenly alarmingly bare. Nothing was there but leftovers from infancy, like "needles and pins, your trouble begins." Or crazily pushing up from below, a line from a Grimm fairy story about the ill-used stepsister who got nothing to eat except crusts until befriended by a magic goat. When she commands, "Little goat bleat, I want to eat," a table springs up, covered with silver dishes steaming with hot, delectable food. Nor was a latter-day memento more to the point, with its "Be good, sweet maid, and let who will be clever; do noble deeds, not dream them all day long," and considering the weight I put on having a mind, it was even hypocritical. I began to suffer from an obscure humiliation, shocked to discover that in a pinch the mind can be swept bare, that thieves have crept in, all unawares, to push out the sublime. The blood could make a fool of the head, and I longed to forget that I had crossed over, or, crossing over, was still so new.

Then I comforted myself. The mind could be a lighthouse, couldn't it? And I would keep my lamp bright. But already it seemed that mine was more like a bicycle lamp, to shed its tiny glimmer along a country road, and I was remembering the night I biked home from a long ride to a farm on the edge of town, where I had gone with two other girls to pick cherries for a farmer who paid us a basketful of cherries for every four baskets we picked for him.

On the way home, the cherry baskets had banged away on our handlebars. But there were as many cherries within as without. Our mouths and hands were pink with the ox-blood juices of the fruit, our gingham dresses stained as if we had knifed the throats of lambs and doves. Climbing the trees on ladders, we perched in the crotch, where the scaly bark crisped to ruffled green moss on the outer side, and on the inner was smooth as silk, warm as a living arm. Above our heads the dark globes of cherries dangled out of reach of our mouths, but pulled down from the bough, the pulp sucked free of its stone spurted its wild juice against the tongue. When dusk came, we set out, pedaling slowly, feeling the weight of our arms and legs. It would have been good to fall down in the ragged grass for a snooze, but dark would soon fall. I remembered it as coming early, with a mass of cloud like a dim mole creeping over a sliver of moon. Then the wayside sprang to life under our bicycle lamps as the outer world fell down. We were alone with our bikes in a little circle of their lights; the weeds along the road lifted tall spiky heads rimmed with the pale rays from our lamps. Silently as robbers we skimmed the dark roads. The candy-stick pink-and-white dress of a girl stuck out against the dark like a barber pole.

Swooping down the last hill and coming to hard pavements with a smack of rubber on asphalt, we took the town by surprise. I was riding ahead.

But the scene was already as detached from me as if I had been watching it slowly evolve in the depths of some crystal ball. On that first day of passing over to the adult side, I was already somebody else. I was shedding my skin and could hear the old skin fall.

A Year of Disgrace

*I*N THE EARLY MONTHS OF THAT YEAR, John Herrmann and I were living in a penthouse on lower Fifth Avenue. The address led visitors from the Midwest to expect elegance. But when a stout uncle from Minneapolis arrived, he refused to budge beyond the second landing and bellowed up the vast stairwell to us, as we leaned down from the top, that he was no Alpine climber. The three rooms perched precariously on top of a solid iron-faced monster, reminding us of the lookout, called a crow's nest, on the high masts of seagoing ships, and during windstorms, with rain battering the windows and hammering on the flat tin roof outside our bedroom, the place shook as we liked to imagine an old windjammer might have shuddered in a gale. The furnishings were sparse. There were six chairs and a round table that trembled to the touch. Two cots covered with plain gray blankets were narrow as a ship's bunk. A dresser, painted black, had six drawers that stuck when you tried to open one in a hurry. In the kitchen, there was a smallish bathtub covered with a lid that served as a table, a washbowl with a cold-water tap, which was also a kitchen sink, and a decrepit gas stove. The toilet was in the outside hallway.

The place was a sublet from a novelist, Leonard Kline, who had retreated to the Connecticut countryside in a last-ditch effort to escape alcoholism but who was to spend a year in the village jail instead. For he had drunkenly chased a visiting friend around his house with a shotgun and killed him. The rent was forty-five dollars a month, and we felt we were lucky to have the place. That it was bare was an advantage. We had a great many books, some in French and German, that we had brought home from Europe two years before. A shop around the corner had dug up some pine boards for us, and we had made bookshelves that gave the main room a look of being lived in. A little model of a Breton fishing boat made out of a solid chunk of oak and fitted with a small square-rigged red sail stood on top of the bookshelves. Painted a dark blue, with its name, *Le Pouldu*, on the prow, it was the first object to strike the eye when you came into the room after the long climb up the six flights of stairs. John had made it during the year we had spent in an old farmhouse in Connecticut.

We had given up our house in Connecticut a few months before, coming to New York in the late fall because our money had run out. After living in Europe, where money had gone a great way, we found that every dollar shrunk from what it had been "over there." But the two of us could still get by in the country for six hundred dollars a year if we took it easy and asked for no more than the essentials. Nobody we knew was out to save for anything except to buy time. If the country was in high-gear prosperity, none of the young people we knew were sharing it. Of all the young writers, Scott Fitzgerald was almost alone in going after money, and he seemed never to have enough.

The owners of the house in the country had magnificently loaned us a big coal stove, bedizened with shiny medals and scrolls of steel. It stood in the living room, where we also slept. We called it the Kaiser. In the dark of night the coal glowed through transparent isinglass doors with the fateful assurance of a charcoal burner's fire in a deep German forest. There was a wood range for cooking in the kitchen and a big pantry stocked with enough to start a small grocery store, for we were three miles from town and had no car. A farmer sold us a quarter of a cow he had butchered, and it hung, during the winter months, frozen stiff as a board in an icy unused room on the second floor. With a saw we could hack off choice cuts for stews or pot roasts. A big ham and a side of bacon were strung on nails from the ceiling of the kitchen. With snow up to the windowsills and the roads a sheet of ripply white where the wind brushed the contours in tiny gusts of drift, we were often as isolated as we might have been on a long voyage beyond sight of land. For a week at a time the mailman, muffled to the eyeballs, in an old buggy drawn by a meek horse breathing frost, could not get through.

With both stoves going and the falling snow blocking the windows inch by inch, we gave ourselves up to the splendors of isolation. During the day we worked at our typewriters, John in the main room, I in the kitchen, where I could keep an eye on the cooking. Dark fell early, and the light from the Aladdin oil lamp cast a mellow glow the color of a ripe pear. With a jug of hard cider drawn from a fifty-gallon keg in our basement, we began to read aloud through the long and wonderful evenings. The reader sat in the one comfortable chair near the lamp, while the listener lay at ease on the big double bed, spread with a bright patchwork quilt. We took turns reading, and it was often two o'clock before we could bear to put the book down. We read Shakespeare's play about Henry at Agincourt and squabbled about Henry's treatment of Falstaff. Or we read the Song of Solomon. A lot of Dickens. Sometimes the next morning at breakfast we would compulsively pick up the book again but break off, guiltily, for a day was for work, not for reading. That winter we read Turgenev's "First Love" and Goncharov's *Oblomov* for the first time, and it is astonishing now, when I think back on it, how we retreated all those snowbound months as one might into a storm cellar, to the literature of the nineteenth century, or pushing on beyond Stendhal, once more involved ourselves with the *Iliad*.

The setting of that room is so vivid, I can see it all, and myself lying on the bed with red slippers dangling from my feet and my head propped upon one hand. I can hear the soft plop of snow on the window and see how the pear-colored light fell on the reader's hands. There were times, when we came to a work I already knew, when I let the words flow over me like water, hearing and not hearing, while some other self burrowed in the dark, sorting out those thoughts that were so manifold and evanescent, or reviewed the past, yesterday or the year before, or speculated on the present. Everything fused, fleetingly, in a flux and ferment, fired by a spark from the words being spoken while you waited, expectant, for the passage that jubilantly intoxicates the heart. The room would stand still, in the shell of a dream, and you hardly dared breathe for fear the spell might be broken. Sometimes late at night a terrifying screech would echo from outside. The first time we heard it we threw open the door, while the snow swirled past us to melt on the floor. The sound was like the cry of a woman in torment, but when we crunched out to see if some human creature had floundered in the drifts, there was only the creak of a broken limb of an old tree, while beyond, high in the night, the demoniac cry echoed again: a screech owl.

On some nights we might spend the hours reading the plays of Heinrich von Kleist or those of Carl Sternheim so we could keep up our German, for we had both spent several years in Germany, I in Berlin, John in Munich. We had met in Paris six months before we were due to sail for home. We met one April evening at the Café du Dôme, on a day I had come up from Italy, and two weeks later we had gone to Le Pouldu, a little town on the coast of Brittany, where Gauguin had once lived and paid for his room with a painting. The way we had met, accidentally, after living in the same country at the same time without crossing paths, seemed one of the marvels of chance events. In the Connecticut farmhouse my thoughts would turn to that summer at the very moment when I would be sitting before my typewriter, and an entire scene from a past time would be suspended before my eyes, enclosed within some magic circle, something apart from any of the life that had gone before or that might ever come again. It was one of the wonders of that isolated winter that nothing one looked at was blocked off in terms of time, and one's mind grew accustomed to work in a particularly ample environment. In terms of space, because the frosty windows and the sweep of snow as bare as a desert floor confined one physically, the ever-present time vistas could come and go, offering a hard stretch of sand on the Brittany coast, where I could see us once more racing in the late afternoon when the fishing boats would be coming home, or, again, walking under the larchwood trees where the light flickered as delicately as shadow birds as we stepped along a leaf-sodden path to Quimperlé. Or a sudden sound would bring straight into the kitchen the creaking of the oars of the fishermen as they rowed down the river to the sea past our hotel at four in the morning under a phantom mist as opaque as old silver, and I would whirl in my chair, startled as though a gun had gone off, to find nothing.

Nor was it only in the daylight of the winter that a scene from another time might push up from the underground. In the depths of night I might wake to hear John call out in muffled German. Or I might wake from a dream where I had been jabbering French, charmed to have heard myself so fluent in a language that in real life, in Paris, had come awkwardly to my tongue. Or I might wake suddenly in dim morning light, in a panic, not knowing in which of the many rooms I had known I now found myself, and in a brief spasm, clutching at now this, now that, or induced by an early fog pasting a clammy damp on the window-panes, retreat back to that room in Seattle where at the end of the Great War the high notes of the Funeral March from Chopin's sonata had pierced to the vitals, for you knew that on the street a long line of hearses was somberly passing, carrying the boys who were dying of flu in the nearby camp to the railroad station with an honor guard, to be shipped back home. In a few brief seconds a host of impressions would whirl wildly as falling leaves, then everything rights, the body beside me was comfortingly there, and the drift had settled down into the autumnal colors of the patchwork quilt that covered us.

In late spring some Connecticut rivers flooded, backed up into inland brooks, and then ebbed, leaving huddles of sticks, old leaves, and the owlish glitter of a tin can. A trickle of young people drifted into the countryside. You could have an abandoned farmhouse for the asking, with little more required than "to fix things up" or to paint a few walls.

Some of the land had been taken over by Polish farmers, whose coarse vitality could better cope with the smitten soil than the tremulous hands of an old New England bachelor, now content with collecting wormy apples for a barrel of hard cider. Katherine Anne Porter rattled around in a stone house in a maple grove, and Nathan Asch scrambled with his wife into a leaky dwelling where a tub to catch the drips was a death trap to the unwary. One day a taxi driving all the way from New York dropped at our door a tall young man in tails, with a wilted white carnation in his buttonhole, and a girl with tawny hair and golden skin, who came toward us in her chiffon evening dress extending one hand from a wrist heavily bandaged. The young man was some-one John had known in Detroit; the girl a showgirl from *George White's Scandals.* They were sick of the messiness of New York, they said, and wanted us to find them a house in the country to live in. Her first account of having cut her wrist "opening a tin can" was changed in a few days to the truth: she had slashed it with a razor blade and had been "a fool." Ted had found her "dripping with gore," had rushed her to a doctor, and at dawn they had walked out into the empty early streets to hail a taxi for the getaway. Ted was an ad writer who vaguely wanted "to write." The girl didn't want to write anything except an occasional letter; she loved making curtains and little dresses, puttering about the kitchen, setting the table. Besides, she was being "written up," so she confided, by "Bunny Wilson, who is putting me in a book." Like everyone else who appears as a character in the work of an author, she didn't think much of it, though she was bursting with pride at being considered a worthy subject. "The way he makes me talk!" she exclaimed. "You'd never believe it!"

But when I came to read *I Thought of Daisy* it seemed

to me that the very exaggerations, of her idiom, for instance, that had repelled the actual Daisy had evoked a protean Daisy as a Leonardo drawing may suggest the image of a woman more provocative than the full-fleshed Gioconda. But I could understand her dismay, perhaps at no more than finding herself in the company of Edna St. Vincent Millay, whose chameleon presence had suggested now a sibyl, now a firebird. But Wilson himself astonished me, emerging in his novel as a sort of Proustian Swann, challenging my first impression of him on an evening when I had gone to see him in his apartment on Washington Square to ask if he would be willing to join a protest against the seizure by the Customs of a novel by John Herrmann, printed by Contact Editions in Paris, and which Morris Ernst had volunteered to defend in the courts. I had been deceived by the plump but graceful figure, the scholar's high brow, the luminous brown eyes, and the face, delicately larded with a baby fat that might never wear off. I had imagined the squire, the don, or, oddly enough, even the choirboy, but not the amorous, complex nature he was attempting to unveil.

And often during that summer, when our house opened from two rooms to six and our garden could have fed a huge family, it seemed to me that each of us in the valley called Merry-all relived some personal adventure as it might have been related in fiction. For surrounded by a company devoted to the art of fiction either as writers or as readers, you felt the source of material of one's own existence stir and come to life, be burnished and glisten, if only for the moment when the faces turned toward you ready to laugh or become bemused. You might be encouraged to ribaldry in recounting some old love affair or in an attempt to be "honest" rob yourself of a subtler truth. One narrator might unconsciously distort for the sake of the paradox, while another might painfully try to trace in the most dissimilar adventures the threads that implied an inner harmony. I might remember the Pears Soap of childhood, its color as translucent as clear quince jelly. Katherine Anne could recall being bathed by the nuns and how the long gown considered appropriate for "modesty's sake" floated out on the bathwater like the pad of a water lily. Or the English painter Ernest Stock might spring a quotation:

When antelopes surmount eagles in flight,
And swans be swifter than hawks of the tower,
Then put women in trust and confidence . . .

thus tempting us to take note of a graver wound than the exterior scars of the shrapnel in his leg, earned in the war when he had been shot down in a plane. As he ran around in shorts, we were not sure he was not trying to expose the one scar in token of the other, but he won no more than comment from a Polish farmwife, who scoffed, "Look at him now, running around in underpants, showing off them bony knees!"

He might drop on the grass to sketch our corncrib, empty except for a mouse, or come suddenly as night fell, pale as an Orestes pursued down the coast of Calabria by the Furies, to beg to spend the night. When I had gone to be upstairs in the dark, I could hear the voices of the men, as they wet their whistles with hard cider in the kitchen, drone on and on. After midnight, they sounded to me as soothing as a guitar played outside the window.

It was an interlude of time as clear and uncertain as a drop of water. It hung, trembling and iridescent, like a fresh green grape. To eat it made a fever in the blood. Should the fever be fed or starved? Where were the sources of energy:

in work, in love, in the ground itself? We could try them all, reaching into the bin that seemed to have no bottom. Sometimes the hands alone held restorative powers and one wished only to be rid of paper. To get close to the sky, skin, taste. To refurnish with a walk at night, or with a wild Polish dance where the shy country women danced, pinching up their stiff skirts in delicate scarred hands. To get up in the morning when the dew frosted the red cabbage, to pounce upon the cutworms ready to wilt the tender pea stalks: what savage energy could leap out at the discovery of the cannibal soon to end his feast between two flat stones! What a miracle currant jelly was, and how I gloated on the little jeweled array of glasses sitting in the sun. Nathan Asch, his hair dabbed with the yellow paint with which he was renovating the interior of his house, found an old waffle iron, scrubbed off the rust, and invited us to waffle feasts with maple syrup. Daisy and Ted went in for pork roasts studded with garlic. Katherine Anne picked a bushel of dandelions to make delicious wine, as subtly intoxicating as champagne. John and Ernest Stock made little models of a Breton fishing boat and competed on a pond with the pomp of a Bermuda race.

Then Ernest persuaded our company to let him pour plaster of Paris around a hand so he could make a cast, which he then filled with some bright silvery substance. When the casts were chipped off, a gallery of oddly assorted hands held out their empty palms. They seemed to be idling for use of the amputated, or destined as offerings to some little shrine where the faithful in thanksgiving for delivery from sudden death bring replicas of a leg or an arm, or hang up a tin miniature heart or lung near the image of a saint.

Detached from myself, I felt my own hand belonged to someone else. Posed like an empty cup, it asked for too much. A counterswing of weather blighted the cucumbers. Opening a dark closet, we found our city shoes greenish white with mildew; long scars had been dragged in our winter clothes by the moths. The apples warned us that summer had ended and that we could no more indulge ourselves with the winy autumn than the cows should have afforded to guzzle the rotting fruit from the ground. A herd came running past our house one afternoon, racing madly from tree to tree, tails flying, a beery foam bearding their muzzles. Gorged on apples under the mile of trees lining the road, beginning to bloat, they were rounded up at last by the desperate farmer, who herded them, drunkenly reeling, bawling piteous cries, past our door. Some died in the night.

The late shimmering of the Queen Anne's lace began to look like frost. Nathan Asch packed his wife off to Duluth, where her father, a rich banker, might be persuaded to give them a loan for the duration of their wait for his novel to be published. Then he hitched a ride to the railroad, with his black cat, Moses, sourly peeping from a basket. Katherine Anne vanished with the mist one early morning on a milk truck. Ted and Daisy, deep in debt for pork roasts and goodies, fled anonymously. Ernest Stock washed his hands of Connecticut, where the landscape had never equaled the downs of England anyhow.

We came back to New York with what we called "the loot": manuscripts of two novels, a basket of currant jelly, and summer tan. No matter what happened, no one could take away what we had made. It might be ground to dust, but it had come alive. It was to take two years before either book saw the light of day, but in the twenties a young writer expected the runaround for a first venture. No one waited for a first novel to be "taken" before beginning new work. Now it was only a question of what next.

We found a room in an old lodging house and went to Julius's place in the Village, which in spite of Prohibition boasted a long bar backed by a high mirror in an elegant walnut frame. John was carrying *Three Lives* with him and had barely laid it down when a man standing next to him, with a soft brown hat jauntily slouched over pale-yellow hair, edged his drink nearer and clearing his throat began, "I see you are carrying Gertie with you." A book like *Three Lives*, a blue-bound contraband *Ulysses*, a copy of *transition* or *This Quarter*, was enough for strangers to strike up a conversation that might lead to the drinking of *Bruderschaft*, a flirtation, or a love affair. Like the speakeasy, a good deal of avant-garde literature was considered unpalatable by the law, and nothing could be more appetizing to the young than the forbidden. That the law was on the side of what the literary left, in its newfound exuberance, called the Philistine made a rallying point for the young for whom freedom to write was synonymous with freedom to love. Nor did it matter that some of the experiments were as obscure as a Chinese ideograph; even the duds generated an atmosphere tingling with the possibility of a chance encounter with the magical phrase. It was with something like pride that the editors of *transition* had announced in Number 7 that Numbers 3, 4, 5, and 6 had been confiscated on grounds of obscenity or other pretexts. Ezra Pound had written that his *Exile One* had been appraised by a Boston customs inspector as "stuff written by some narcotic fiend. Nobody has thoughts like those except under the influence of drugs." Brancusi's sculpture was taxed by the Port of New York on the ground that it "wasn't sculpture but metal." A few weeks later they passed in the Hope diamond free, on the ground that it was a work of art.

Holger Cahill knew just the place for us; he even had

the key to the sublet on Fifth Avenue. We promptly walked around to look the place over, climbed the six flights of stairs, and agreed at once that it was a regular crow's nest and just the thing. Cahill was living in a "corner" of a loft on Fourteenth Street. The loft, big as a skating rink, had been taken by a young couple, friends of his, who had fitted it with tall screens separating living from sleeping quarters, a potbellied stove on an apron of zinc, pots of ivy at the windows; they, in turn, had taken Cahill in. He had transformed it in his imagination to a Dostoevskian "corner" and fairly gloated on his situation; temporary, of course, until the suitable thing turned up. Like everyone else we came to know that winter, he had come from somewhere else. His young boyhood on the plains of North Dakota had been his nemesis: the arched blue sky, the wavering sea of wheat unbroken by the spar of a single tree. Family disasters had pitched him to wandering; he had bummed rides on trains, met up with migratory IWW farmhands and tramps of the jungle, hit midwest cities and worked on small-town papers, inching his way, nibbling his education from books and papers, chewing his destiny fine, and, burned up with curiosity, stung by the itch to see it all, to know it all, had managed to get himself to China, where his imagination had been taken over as the imaginations of others may be taken over by the Greeks or Etruscans. In New York he had filled in his sketchy education at the Rand School, at Columbia, at Cooper Union. Through his contact with social critics like Thorstein Veblen and Horace Kallen, he began to fuse his native talents with his experience, and now, though an assistant to John Cotton Dana at the Newark Museum, he had found time to write a first novel, soon to be published. He was complaining that night that most writers were ignoramuses on the subject of art unless like E. E. Cummings they could draw or like John Dos Passos painted watercolors in the manner of *Manhattan Transfer*. As for most painters, they blacked out when it came to literature, he said, adding mournfully, "We have no Apollinaires, no Baudelaires." He might have added, "We have no cafés," for the speakeasies, with their heavy white cups holding dago red, hardly filled the bill.

I don't suppose all of his story came out on the first evening. But it was a mark of the time and the place that a first encounter might last all night, overflowing from the speakeasy to the street, from the street to someone's room, to pitch you finally into a dawn exhilarated, oddly at peace, for wasn't it of engagements like this, long talks and walks, that you had dreamed in the midwest town before the war when the sky had pressed above your head like a burnished brass bowl and the long secretive dark express trains zipped into the horizon? You had dreamed of it as surely as you had dreamed of love. A book told you it was so, long before you had the chance to prove it, when some knowing librarian, seeing you flounder in the bookstacks, had put into your hand books beyond your years to prove to you, beyond the shadow of a doubt, that explosive, wonderful, witty talk existed somewhere as surely as it did in the pages of *The Way of All Flesh, Sanine,* or *Madame Bovary*. More than the theater, or the bright thoroughfares of big towns, more than the chance to see "real" paintings in big galleries, was the hope to verify the book by the human encounter.

Perhaps it was in those early days, in the little town, that "the word" had come to seem a holy thing. But "the word" can be used or misused by anyone. It can be flogged to death. Common denominator though it be, it may become the little stick of dynamite. It can drown the brook in a rumbling mountainside. We saw it happen. The Great

War began in 1914 with no more than the incredulity of the elders—"Why, they can't let it go on. It's barbarism"—but led right on through muddled unwillingness, to sluggish hesitation, to jingoist cries, to rhetorical betrayals; until beneath the public harangues other voices spoke and you heard them: D. H. Lawrence, Barbusse, Romain Rolland, Emma Goldman, John Reed—dissenters, dissenting among themselves but reminding you that what you hoped to live for lived. An underground aliveness burned and stirred, made signals in the dark.

A good deal of social existence eddied around "corners" where in little nests scooped out of old tenements, in basements, the newly arrived youth had stripped themselves to modest requirements. Though we had put distance between ourselves and our origins, and now, as through a telescope, imagined we might view the planets that had presided at our birth, we bore the stigmata of an early upbringing. It would take years to value the long shadows on the grass, the smell of homemade bread, the hum of telegraph wires in the winds of an empty prairie. Now we chose to remember the rustling long skirts, the heavily flowered hats, of mothers or older sisters whose tiny pinched waists had betrayed the stays of a cruel medieval corset and whose notions of beauty might lead to an elegant vase from Tiffany, where, under the spell of an artful design, the true functions of a rose were lost in the whorls of an erotic daydream. So the sword of Picasso's analytical cubism had ripped the plump cushions on those enormous divans that had suggested, but only suggested, a harem, for the stiff braided designs, the heavy knots of beads and sequins, could only invite a mystique that seized on the erotic as a defense against life, not as an invitation. "The lovely and the beautiful" became for our generation a term of contempt; the grounds for complacency held by the parents, despised. As the Paris Surrealists had discarded Anatole France for a more distant Lautréamont or Rimbaud, some of us pried open the Pandora box of the past to see what had once lived there. You might rescue the old daguerreotype of a great-uncle whose bold profile of the arrogant black sheep was more seductive than the direct gaze of a grandfather seated in a genteel armchair, his hand on a Bible. Cahill discovered his Icelandic forebears to be more fertile to his imagination than his father, who had deserted his mother, or his mother, who had seemed to desert him when she married again.

Nor had all the newcomers flocked from the Midwest; some had moved up from the South. Allen Tate and Caroline Gordon held out in a basement apartment on Bank Street with rent free in return for janitor service. Allen stoked the furnace, while Caroline looked after the stairs and hallways, hiring neighborhood colored women to scrub and clean. Ford Madox Ford's imposing white walrus presence was stationed on the top floor, where a fireplace burned chunks of coal all day long. Besides writing, keeping their apartment tidy, and cooking, Caroline acted as secretary for Ford that winter and even found time for a stray job of editing or proofreading. Like the rest of us, she was ready to try her hand at anything.

Katherine Anne Porter was living on the third floor of a rickety house on Hudson Street, called by its witty tenants Casa Caligari. Creaking up the stairs, you half expected to see a skeleton wag from the ceiling, but instead a door opened on the second landing to a view of a child strapped to a high chair while it gobbled its bowl of bread and milk. It was Dorothy Day's little daughter, a rare sight, for children were few and far between for our generation. When you came to Katherine Anne's room the prospect opened surprisingly to a domestic pavilion with gingham curtains at a window, a flowering primrose, a small cookstove with a coffeepot sizzling away, a gray cat on a cushion in a child's rocking chair. Her footing was as precarious as the house was shaky, but she could make light of it, wittily tossing the jacket of a book she had reviewed into a wastebasket or pinning up the jacket of Holger Cahill's *Pagan Earth*, with a drawing by John Sloan, in a place of honor. She was promising herself to do a review of the book, but she never got around to it.

Nor did we get around to many of the things we had promised ourselves we would do when, in the country, we had taken a long view of the time to come. Brute necessity gobbled up time and energy. With no money, we had taken the first jobs that had been offered. John had a wardrobe that might have qualified him for a "young executive," as his well-to-do father sent him custom-made suits of the finest British material. My once smart Paris clothes were no longer so smart but would do for hanging around big laundries to get information from the working girls about their "conditions" for a research outfit. I could laugh at myself as a "big collar-and-cuff" woman, but selling books at Brentano's rubbed your nose into the fact that the best-sellers might be no more than best-sellers. In the grip of making ends meet, everyone was compelled to commit follies. Down to ten dollars, I could throw it away on a delectable hat. Katherine Anne Porter invested in a chair with a delicate frame and a striped upholstery of blue-and-lilac-veined satiny material that gouged a hole in her "capital" bigger than what remained. A young man might phone his girl, "I'll bring you asparagus in a taxi." A youth with literary aspirations, freshly out of college, might decide to have a grand fling before settling down to brass tacks, and, with no other obligations than to salute the captain of a cattle boat, reporting hourly, "The cattle are all well, sir," get a comfortable bunk with good victuals, ten days' sail on the high seas, and a week in Paris.

Mobility not only was in the blood but was a fact. The youthful juices had neither jellied nor atrophied, and if some of the young played with the recklessness of a gambler, with no more of a stake than talent and a fanatic's will, if the risks were high, what did you lose? The bottom had dropped out of the old world, and it was a truism that the "old men had not only bungled the peace" but screwed up the works. President Harding had been a stooge, the highest government officials had been crooks, and Coolidge, lulled by a booming stock market, took long naps every afternoon in the White House. The biggest city in the world had a playboy for mayor, who had danced the cancan in a homosexual dive in Berlin. Disenchantment was not only a necessity, it was a joy.

It was in this kind of setting that the early stories of Hemingway—then playing a lone hand in Paris—made so grave a mark. His young Nick might be the remains of the solitary trapper, but now he was educated, and through with everything, nourishing the residual grit of anarchism as a last hope. Don't get held by anything. Avoid getting connected. Break it up. What a pleasure! His young love ends: "It isn't fun any more. . . ." "Everything's gone to hell inside me." It was really honest. Don't be sentimental and hold on to something that is dead. Beat it.

Every generation wants to be spoken to in its own terms. Young people of the twenties had been brought up in schools and universities where contemporary literature was a buried subject. You were given Longfellow and Whittier rather than Whitman. Who had heard of Melville until

Raymond Weaver of Columbia began to unearth him in the twenties? But provincial towns had taken education seriously, had made impassioned readers of those with the inclination; we knew the classics, read Virgil in Latin, knew Plato and, if not Greek, the translations. We had acquired taste through mad love, an extracurricular hit-and-miss encounter that had skinned and scarred and set a mark upon the forehead. We knew we were in a period of evolution and called it a transitional time. What period is not in transition? We named it as if it had never happened before, feeling ourselves actors in a rare moment, caught in a situation that would require not only flexibility but intensity of purpose. If more of the young were involved in an artistic movement than in political awareness, it was because politics had not yet put the bite on. Who believed in the vote? Women had been given the vote, but if they were now "emancipated," it was not through suffrage but by jobs, birth control, even Prohibition. If a fine material spirit existed between the sexes, it was a tonic and a splendor after so much sticky intermingling and backboneless worship of the family and domesticated bliss. We were a stiff-necked generation, defiant, each ready to defend his side, her side, against assault. You had to stand up for yourself, in literature as in love, and both worlds at their best had a wild salty savor.

A sense of fatalism fed the anarchistic heart, but fatalism does not always degrade. It may inspire elation. A pessimistic outlook was countered by a buoyant confidence in the precious moment. If we had abandoned the safe lives our parents had fancied so valuable, we seemed to have gained an insight into the creative fissures of the world. The fires and smoke steamed up from volcanoes, old and new. What had Baudelaire *really* said? Was Poe a phony? Stendhal, newly translated in the twenties, became a contemporary: a

73

young man speaking for the age. A young writer in New York might hang a death mask of Nietzsche on the wall, remembering that young Russian poet in mittens and overcoat who had scribbled away beneath his freezing death mask of Pushkin.

The little magazines, so different from the academic organs they were to become, tempted, teased, provoked, and ridiculed. The editors of *The Little Review* might publicly disagree, one stating that Hart Crane had better drop dead, the other claiming him as the finest of the hour. Irresponsible in any academic sense, the little magazines steered wildly, invited hugely, and didn't care a rap if they printed a shapeless imitation of Joyce by a youngster from Davenport alongside a hunk of the actual Joyce. A writer might flit with ease from the pages of *The Little Review* to *The Dial* or on the same day send one manuscript to *transition* and another to H. L. Mencken. Or be aware that in the publishing house of Charles Scribner's Sons, Maxwell Perkins would be sorting the wheat from the chaff and, reading the little magazines, would know your name before he knew you. Whether it was the more solid, dignified *Dial,* whether it was the little magazine, the stage was set for an international set of players; the era that gave the Model T Ford to the farmers opened the world to its literary young on a scale never before ventured and not equaled since.

Ungratefully, rudely, some of the young made a swift bypass around their immediate literary progenitors, skirting Anderson and Dreiser in search of the unknown. In France the Surrealists had brutally ditched the "sugary" Anatole France; in Russia the process had begun earlier, and four young writers of whom Mayakovsky was one had delivered their manifesto, "A Slap in the Face of Public Taste." Delivered with all the confidence of youth and with youth's delight in shocking its elders, it had advised its readers, among other things:

> Throw Pushkin, Dostoevsky, Tolstoy, etc., overboard from the steamer of modernity.

> He who will not forget his first love will not recognize his last.

> All these Maxim Gorkys, Bloks, Sologubs, Remizovs, Chernys, etc., etc.—all they want is a villa by the river. That is how fate rewards tailors.

And in the same mood it was a pleasure to chant:

> There's not a single gray hair in my soul;
> With nice old men I have nothing to do!
> The world shakes with my voice's roll,
> And I walk handsome
> And twenty-two.

Or, stimulated by a flaming punchino, some of us might recite in unison the maddening, repetitive lines from Kurt Schwitters's "Revolution in Revon," beginning with "Mama, the man is standing there" and ending with "They must be curious trees indeed, where the big elephants go walking, without bumping each other!" Or reel off the intoxicating Dadaist verse of Hans Arp (later to become Jean Arp), whom we familiarly referred to as "the trap drummer."

Literature had not yet been boxed off from life. Nor had a body of critics nominated themselves as "the elite." You might write reviews for the literary supplements without having to qualify as a professor. A good deal of reviewing was done by practicing writers; painters like Léger and

Picasso, Max Ernst and Klee, explained themselves. The reader had not yet been herded to pastures chosen for him by the book clubs, nor did toplofty foundations presume to supervise culture from a doubtful pinnacle. The young writer had a private life, where he could grow, change, develop. Or quit. You might not be a Dante; but Dante was dead. Your milieu was your own, and nobody who was not alive could say the special words that needed saying to interpret it. You discovered on your own the worthy dead, without the aid of scholars, who also had not yet begun to gang up on the living.

With fingerprinting, the image of man dwindled to the guilty worm, but in the twenties we still were able to discern something of the divine. Two young people writing in different styles, using different materials, could afford hospitality to one another's work. Those who had socialist inclinations, those who ran gaily down the stairs with a manuscript no one would ever print, those who liked to read "The Waste Land" aloud to a girl, even though she fell asleep, those who were oddballs, those who fancied that the wits of the Algonquin were reincarnations of the eighteenth-century London coffeehouse customers—all mingled in a sort of ridiculous, gorgeous, open-house limbo. Young women who in an earlier era might be getting the kids ready for school fancied themselves as Aspasias and counted the number of their "affairs" as their mothers might have added up the household linen. Without a reader's guide, you could make what you pleased of a sentence from Joyce: "What bird has done yesterday man may do next year, be it fly, be it moult, be it agreement in the nesto," or you could relish plain lines by Alexander Blok: "Excuse me sir, we don't allow that. You're picking over all the crayfish. No one will eat them." We could even suffer with laughter the tortured exercises of some of our contemporaries, who, intoxicated with Joyce or under the spell of Freud, examined minutely their own often quite uninteresting interiors.

Pound could afford a worldview that in 1927 would advise: "Lenin is more interesting than any surviving stylist. He probably never wrote a single brilliant sentence; he quite possibly never wrote anything an academic would consider a 'good sentence,' but he invented or very nearly invented a new medium, something between speech and action (language as cathode ray) which is worth any writer's study."

But you had to eat. Pay rent. Nobody thought then of leaving the university in order to dive back into it as an instructor. Pound, aided and abetted by Mencken, had presented the academic world as a Black Hole of Calcutta. Better to try your luck on Wall Street selling bonds. When neither the Brentano job nor my laundry enterprise proved enough to keep us afloat, John left the city as a traveling salesman for a publishing house on the big short trip to Midwest cities, and I landed a job reading for a pulp-magazine outfit.

There were a dozen magazines going full blast, a dozen editors, a dozen desks, a dozen bottles of bootleg gin concealed in a lower drawer. You had to have the stuff to wade through the day. Our publisher liked to remind his employees, some of whom were bright boys out of Yale and Princeton, that there were advantages to be had beyond the stipend, and with the air of a big foundation establishing a fellowship, held up Dreiser and other "big names" who had made a start in similar enterprises. When the visiting authors, curiously prim, elderly bodies, who wrote with lubricity about chorus girls and Rotarians on the loose, complained that the editors interviewed them "reeking with gin," we were scolded by our publisher and forced to add peppermint drops and cloves to the bottom-drawer arsenal.

Cooped up in a small office with a meek woman in black who read for a true-confession magazine, I might mix up her monologue with the manuscript I was trying to read and suddenly feel that I had fallen into a bear trap where the stinging bottle flies of words, written or spoken, were the real menace. Nothing could stop her; her voice was the voice of an endless soap opera that now and then disengaged itself from a recount of her love life with a Japanese "poet" to sing of the virtues of Katherine Mansfield, whom she was studying seriously, so she said, for that day of days when she would ditch all this for her "own work." And as if to prove her claim that she could write, she might drift into a descriptive passage, filled with periods and semicolons, dashes and pauses, and in which she offered herself as a crucified relic of love with the flourish of Brutus extolling the death of Caesar.

But is there such a thing as the twenties? The decade simply falls apart upon examination into crumbs and pieces which completely contradict each other in their essences. The twenties was not at all the museum piece it has since become, where our literary curators have posed on elevated pedestals a few busts of the eminent. Even individual characters cannot be studied in a state of static immobility. It was all flux and change, with artistic movements evolving into political crises, and ideas of social service, justice, and religious reaction had their special spokesmen. You might be invited to look forward to the social millennium or to the mechanical millennium; you might beat a retreat to Jeffersonian agrarianism. Mencken and Pound could exchange insults and compliments, Mike Gold of the *New Masses* lunch amiably with an editor of the *New Republic*. Ernest Boyd might travesty the new poets for Mencken, but the new poets were not defenseless and, in a body as committed to their intentions as the Surrealists were to their idea of Infinity, held together for attack and pursuit, even contemplating vengeance of another order, for Allen Tate was of the opinion that verbal reply was too honorable and that it would serve Mencken right to be dealt with as a scoundrel, waylaid in the dark and beaten up in a dark alley.

Styles in manners had shifted as well as styles in women's clothing since the early days of the twenties. By 1927 you could make two dresses of the material it would formerly have taken to make one. Hats with brims became helmets out of which the face pressed, egglike, from a nest too tight. What had happened to early friends to whose inspired account of Nijinsky you had listened respectfully? The swan of Pavlova, the incomparable, had evolved to other swans, and the oldsters who with moist eyes affirmed that the great artists were vanishing, were bores. How could that be when *Jurgen* had given way to Joyce and Proust? And what did you care for Eliot's pronouncement that the novel was dead? It was as tiresome as the premature announcement of Lenin's death had been. At that very moment, an ear to the underground could hear the murmur of new voices, or catch D. H. Lawrence in flight.

The very stuff of conversations had shifted. In the early twenties, before I went to Germany, I had often visited the apartment of Alex Gumberg on Union Square, where the talk veered around the Russian Revolution and the civil war; where the heroes were Lenin and Raymond Robins. Now, in 1927, on my way home from the pulp mill I might drop by at the Tates', and standing in the doorway listen idly to the conversation that went on uninterrupted by a new presence, and wonder just which war was being discussed. But in a few moments a name would flash and I knew this was our Civil War; the heroes Lee and Stonewall Jackson.

Or I might come upon a poker game in the same apartment, during which Allen would be wearing "for luck" a wide-brimmed black hat that looked to me suitable for a Kentucky colonel, and Hart Crane, glancing briefly from the cards in his hand, flashed a beam from blue eyes that made his upstanding brush of white hair seem to belong to another man. Malcolm Cowley, with the rosy face of a farm boy, down for the day, drawled a hello, as Caroline darted from the kitchen, where she had just torn their big yellow cat from the lamb chops freshly delivered by the butcher boy. Some of the young people who had lived abroad liked to talk of their days in Europe as an expatriate adventure, but the real expatriates were the southerners in New York, who came with a bloom of other lands more remote than modern France with its bright band of Paris Surrealists in their blue suits and white ties, their nonexistent means of livelihood, their pursuit of the mystical experience—"eager to discover the formula and the place." The Surrealists were even a sort of seismograph vibrating not only to the unseen but to the underground tremors of an explosion to come. But the southerners reminded you of the fluctuations of time, and coming upon Allen Tate, suddenly, as he sat in his apartment without seeing you arrive, you seemed to be looking at a figure, enhanced by a fair skin and a noble bulging forehead, that could have belonged to an exiled dauphin of France, dreaming of the forfeits history had demanded. Caroline, sweeping by, with an energy that stifled the air, touching with a quick hand now a cat, now a book, imposed upon your imagination some grandmother who had once had her hands full with a thousand supervisory chores and had stood looking out over plowed acres with the authority of a commander.

But if you passed the Tates' door and mounted the stairs to the apartment where Ford lived, you might enter his place to a voice murmuring and come upon Ford sitting in an armchair, with his bare feet in a steaming footbath, while before him stooped the slight, delicate form of Biala, his adored companion, who, forgetting her own painting, commiserated in tender tones, "Oh, the poor feet," as she laved the misshapen bunions and broken arches of a man whose voice, often wheezing and whistling, reminded you of the poison gas and the trenches of a war our generation thought it could never sufficiently remember. And the presence of Ford, sitting stoutly erect, his florid face illuminated by pale-blue eyes and furnished with a little mustache sometimes military, sometimes straggling, was so real and so of the world that passing down the stairs again, you hardly stopped at that other door, where some charming ambassador from the South might have newly arrived: Robert Penn Warren, very slim, with a plume of red hair, or Andrew Lytle, a squire from the eighteenth century, sandy, bemused.

For Ford could remind you by a poignant presence of the price you paid, not only for war, but to be alive. And with that reminder I could stiffen myself for the long climb to our crow's nest, where I now kept a solitary vigil, and see the little boat *Le Pouldu*, with its sail drooping, as a puny but indestructible adversary to that other boat, pictured in a reproduction called *Au Bord de la Mer*, by de' Chirico, which I had pinned to the wall, and where a classic archway opens only to space and the sky holds a cluster of pearly clouds that might be no more than the puffs from a shell exploded from the futuristic battleship posed naked on the dry land of an empty quay.

It was not always your contemporaries who reminded

you of your contemporary world. Nor, though you might snatch at a new *transition* as a member of an underground might pore over a secret leaflet for a possible direction to action, could you always respond with a throb of conviction. There was a scatterbrained diffusiveness about some of these outpourings that aroused suspicion. Was modernity becoming a cult? Could "the word" become an idolatrous symbol of the inane? But a single issue might mingle sense with sensibility, or pose questions that forced sterner answers than the question might imply. Reading the editors' "Revolt of the Philistine," you might agree, without exactly knowing why, that it was, indeed, a "year of disgrace."

"The Philistine is as much the serf of living forces around him as ever," the editorial ran. "Dominated by his egotism and his sentimentality, he is incapable of hatred or love. He is not interested in the arts, save in their scandals. Dully he travels through his little world, devoid of any fresh impulse, hypocritically ecstatic at cultural phenomena, and, after his little sensation, goes back to his cocktail swilling and his self-sufficiency. His loves are whoremongering impulses, for he lacks the courage of his emotions."

In April John came home. He looked thin, his dark eyes enormous in a paper-white face, but he was jubilant. He had stopped off at his hometown in Michigan, where he had acquired another unnecessary suit and had, at his mother's insistence, seen a doctor. "I'm a wreck," he said joyfully, laughing as I had once seen him laugh at the Fratellini clowns in Paris. "Is it something to laugh at? What do you mean?" I asked him coldly, for I was terrified. "Yes," he said calmly. "It is: (a) I am a wreck—my blood is thinning to water; (b) I have to take a long vacation; (c) we go to Maine and buy a boat. I know just the place. This trip was good; the haul was good. We can do it."

So we took misfortune to be a godsend, and as if to send us off with trumpets, the long heralded premiere of George Antheil's *Ballet Mécanique* occurred at the Carnegie shortly before our departure. The Antheil performance was a signal for the gathering of the clan. Pound had been beating the drum for the young composer for years, and in 1924, in Paris, we had been present at a private concert where Joyce, in dark glasses, half reclined in a long chair, conspicuously set apart from its fellows. Eyes were upon him when, at the close, the composer sat modestly, his hands in his lap, while Joyce lifted two long pale hands and, extending them at arms' length, began a slow clapping that was the signal for the younger members of the audience to break out into wild applause. If the frantic response had struck me as comic, it might have been because the music had merely stirred me to confused wonderment. But my lack of enthusiasm didn't prevent me from wanting to attend the Carnegie performance.

We had spent that Sunday afternoon on Long Island Sound, sailing in the thirty-five-foot Alden ketch of our friends John and Liza Dallet. A contrary wind had delayed our landing, and there was no time to rush home to change clothes before the concert. We had not bought tickets in advance but were now glad of it, as we were hardly dressed suitably for anything but standing room. With our hair windblown, in sweaters, mine spotted where coffee had spilled upon it, we stood eagerly at the rear of the auditorium, where we could watch the well-dressed audience, some of whom were smiling small patronizing grimaces as they fluttered their programs. Antheil looked wonderfully youthful, with pale bangs cut straight above level eyebrows, as he sat erect before one of the jumbo pianos in a company that presently broke into a din of saxophones, xylophones, trombones, drums, evoking a maddened collision of braying steamboats, screeching factory whistles, with a yelp of human joy wriggling through a murderous crash of cymbals. The sound stunned the senses. A gentleman in formal attire rose from his seat and, hoisting a cane to which he had tied a white handkerchief, began a slow and insulting exit. Titters broke out, followed by indignant hisses from the faithful. The performance closed to thunderous applause, hoots, catcalls. One dignified customer with white whiskers waddled majestically up the aisle, braying lustily. The audience milled in the lobby; reporters darted about, buttonholing Nathan Asch, who, in dark formal clothes, proudly refused to answer questions, saying with a smile of lofty modesty, "I don't care to make a statement. I'm part of the movement." William Carlos Williams, in from Rutherford, grabbed John's arm, insisting we must come backstage and say a word to Antheil. And meet Pound's parents, who had come, loyally, all the way from Idaho for the occasion. The green room was choked with enthusiastic cohorts, but I only remember Pound's parents, two frail, beautiful old people with white hair, both very slender, with spots of bright color in their cheeks, who stood shaking hands as if they had been parents at the wedding reception of a favorite son.

What did the music mean? I longed to be moved as all our friends seemed to be, including John, but it seemed to me I had heard no more than a hallelujah to the very forces I feared. My longing for a still, small voice, for a spokesman not for the crash of breakers on the rock but for the currents, down under, that no eye could see, made me feel alone but not an alien, and I looked at John, too, coldly, as one who had joined forces with some mysterious enemy. Was Antheil to be the symbol of an opposition to the Philistine? In a corner of my heart a slow movement of the pulse began to turn my attention elsewhere.

We were not to depart on the receding waves of sound from the Antheil concert, however, but on a far more somber note. On April 9, the sentence of death had been finally and irrevocably passed on the avowed anarchists Sacco and Vanzetti, imprisoned seven years. What had we expected, those of us who could not believe in their guilt? At the start, only a nucleus, such as had formed around Dreyfus, had persisted, broken into factions, re-formed, persevered, until gradually through the years a widening breach in an impassive society had brought many people of assorted temperaments, beliefs, backgrounds, and convictions to the conclusion that the fish peddler and the cobbler were innocent of the crimes of which they had been accused. Who can tell the source of a belief that may be concealed from the believer? So some who might never have been presumed to care were first caught, as by a flying thistledown, when they heard that Vanzetti was reading Dante's *Vita Nuova* in his prison cell. The prisoners' hunger strikes might have stirred a man who could remember the Irish rebellion. Did the seashells Vanzetti liked to hold in his hands call to some? Or his words?: "Nothing is worse than false belief of self-goodness or greatness. It is that which permitted Nero to kill his mother without remorse."

But in Maine, only the twenty-three-foot ketch that John named the *Josy* counted. It had been a ship's longboat, fifty years old, a double-ender, of stout oak, which we had picked up in a shipyard at Boothbay Harbor, fitted with masts, a red mainsail, a white jig and jigger. An old sea captain who had sailed to the Banks in a Gloucester fishing schooner for fifty years had built a cabin on her and had rented us his own tiny house, modeled like a ship, with a galley, a main room with a five-pointed mariner's star on the ceiling, a cookstove, and two small staterooms with built-in bunks. He had decided to give up his house to us on the day he found out that we adhered to sail, not power, and, taking a few dented pots, a handful of shabby coats, and a long flannel nightshirt, had marched off to "bach it" in an empty neighboring house, from which he could supervise all our seagoing activities. The little house was so skeletal, so trim, so smudged with human usage, its walls so deeply ingrained with the smoke from hundreds of fish frying and the fumes from the kerosene lamps, that it was like a ship long hardened to weather, ready to ride a gale or float upon the night, far out on the steadiness of an empty sea.

For someone like myself, born inland, never so happy as when crumbling earth with my hands for the planting of seeds, the sea and the waters emptying into it offered an occult science. But John had been sailing small craft on Lake Michigan all his life, could read the esoteric language of a chart, and knew navigation. And for months before we made the voyage in outside waters that was to terminate in the port of New York, our daily journeyings back and forth on smaller ventures, to Boothbay or Wiscasset or beyond to Monhegan Island, required the careful study of the tides— no longer a picturesque seething of water against rocks but a signal to come or go. You had to wait for the moment when you might float home on the tide's dark swell under a full moon as you had to halt on land when a black cloud, no bigger than a great bird, gave the secret sign though the sky was blue. Nor could you play tricks with the sea. Like someone taught never to point a gun at anyone even though it is not loaded, we studied the water and skies with respect. The ketch was tiny, had no power, but neither power nor bigness mattered. Seaworthiness was all. The *Titanic* had foundered; the *Josy* could ride out a gale. And to back up his assurance, not for himself but for me, John had the lore of small craft in his memory, could recite names and dates: how Captain Slocum, single-handed, had sailed his sloop around the world; how a frail tall-masted bark had clawed out a hurricane with master and mate lashed to the rigging.

And in May, when it was reported that a young man flying solitary in a tiny aircraft might be passing directly over us on the long flight to Paris, we and the farmers in their fields watched the sky, bemused by a gull, once deceived by a local plane that, dizzied with the course plotted over the Atlantic, swooped and whooped over our heads like a small boy at the edge of a ball field where his hero is making a home run. When the news came that Lindbergh had landed at Le Bourget, the joy was contagious. The fish peddler delivering our mackerel gave a little prance to show that the wings of Mercury were in his heels; a farmer stopping in his field to hoist his plow, stuck in the mire, stroked the shiny blade as he might a plane's propeller. We, too, were thrilled. Were not a bird of the air and a small black leaf floating on the water contiguous?

A new kind of world had opened up; a new lingo. The old Captain could sit on a mossy bank mending a fishnet while he recovered his lost voyages, where the ice had frozen on the halyards as thick as your arm. He could call back his wives: one divorced, one dead. And he could spit, with a careful wiping of his straggling mustache, delicately colored with chewing tobacco, as he discounted the appraisal of the landlubbers who thought it folly for us to make the attempt down the coast in "that tiny boat with no power." "Always trust sail," the Captain said. "She'll ride like a gull. A seaworthy craft. Power can leave you helpless as a bug in midocean. Why, you can't even shake hands with the captain of a power boat; they're too dirty."

What couldn't the Captain's hands do! They were small, brown, and flexible. The tips of the fingers felt like velvet; the cords on the backs of the hands could thong out in spurts of energy or lie supine under knotted blue veins. The handclasp was oddly gentle; a confiding giving that let the hand lie in yours a second, with a modest pressure upon withdrawal. Attacking a fish, his hands flashed with a quick jab of the knife he always carried with him in an oiled leather sheath. Never go without a knife. Never go without chawing tobacco. Keep matches dry. Though he was eighty years old, "widder women" were still after him, he boasted, eyes twinkling, an amorous gleam fondling the hull of the sleek black *Josy.* On a joint expedition to Monhegan, his little sloop, frail as a matchbox, could outride the *Josy* by virtue of his skill. Or he might stand outside on a morning after I had washed all the windows of his house, waiting for me to come out to call, "You got her shined up like a lighthouse. Saw your light last night from way up the road. Could sail by that beam, you could."

We might walk to the river's edge on a dark night for nothing more than to see how bright our light was, how truly like a lighthouse, and how pleasant to follow its long delicate beam where it tangled in the grass down the hillside, beckoning us home. In other ways the house had a magnetic quality; it could attract to us forgotten images, mislaid incidents, and bring flying through the air odd assortments from the past. John might remember the old fellow who had kept a bicycle shop where flyblown postcards of a lady in bloomers paddling for dear life on a bike named "Tiger" and a couple seated on a tandem provided a picture gallery the kids never tired of staring at, and how he had once astonished them by taking an opera hat out of a pasteboard box, advising them to touch it and see if it was not as "sleek as a seal." Or I might find myself recounting how my younger sister and I used to walk in the rain in Seattle during the war and how one night she stopped, the conversation died, as she put the question for which I knew no answer: "What would you do if your husband came home *in a basket*?" For what possible extremity were we preparing ourselves? Was a leg-less husband the worst that might happen? In the Captain's house it was awesome to sort out the bits of drift that floated out from other days, to piece together this with that and to feel a rush of blood to the head with the complexity of the material, its richness, its mystery. Or to wonder how to make it come alive in words, in what pattern, what form. John might confess that he wasn't really a *von* Herrmann, as he had first claimed in Paris, but only Herrmann, or we might laugh ourselves silly remembering the time he had introduced me to a fellow Detroiter with the remark that I had "been with Mencken," intending to refer to the two years I had read manuscripts on the old *Smart Set,* and how his friend, not to be outdone in sophistication, had leaped at the notion that I had been not a reader but a mistress.

Or we might wish we had brought more books with us and fishing in our memories be chagrined that we could bring up the last lines of Cowper's "On the Death of Mrs. Throckmorton's Bullfinch" but not Hamlet's soliloquy. On an evening when the Captain might drop in for some boot-leg beer, John magnificently recited with dramatic effect the ballad beginning: "A bunch of the boys was whooping it up in the Malamut saloon." The room would take on the liveli-ness of a theater, with the Captain now and then politely opening the door to eject a long squirt of tobacco juice into the outer darkness. He was once inspired to contribute himself, resurrecting ten stanzas ending with:

> And I would give all my greenbacks
> For those bright days of yore
> When little Nellie Gray and I
> Slid down the cellar door.

There were moments when the Captain, with his bright blue eyes, reminded me of my mother, only to have her fade in what seemed to be an impersonation of my father, who had taken me to the train when I was bent on leaving home, saying simply, with utter trust, "Jo, I don't know what you're after, but I wish you all the luck in the world." The Captain, too, wished us all the luck in the world, though he might not follow us into that outer space where we would be shortly going. For we had to part. It was coming to mid-August; the season for good sailing down the coast would soon be ended. We hauled up the last lobster pot, cooked the six beauties in the iron tub in the yard to a brilliant red. The acrid smoke stung the eyes, hung on the air with a pungent piny fragrance. The Captain shared our last meal with us, while we poured the melted butter on and broke open the last bootleg beer. The lamp chimneys shone from a last washing in soapsuds. The floor had been scrubbed. "Why, I don't know what to make of my house," mooned the Captain. "It's clean as a bread knife."

The *Josy* was lying in the Sheepscot, loaded, ready to go. We boarded to make a last-minute check of our equipment. A roll of charts to cover the voyage down the coast; the one covering the first leg of our trip was laid out, ready for use. The Coastal Guide was in its rack. The compass, the foghorn, the anchor. A can of kerosene to fuel the riding lights. A powerful flashlight. Fishing tackle and a net. A homemade bobbin of wood to mend the net, smooth and polished by hand, with *Josy* carved in the shank. A life jacket for me, stowed in the cockpit. A collapsible stove called Not-a-Bolt, to set up for outdoor cooking in the cockpit; a foot-square, sheet-iron cube, with a pipe to puff the smoke away, it was a wonderful sight cooking an omelet, frying ham and eggs, or boiling potatoes. The dinghy held a pile of kindling wood, split fine for a quick fire; an old raincoat kept the wood dry. A Sterno for use in the cabin in bad weather. Clothes were crammed into a sailor's seabag. We both had seagoing slickers and were going to need them. Our gear was stored in the forward hold or under our bunks. The bunks were spread with woolen blankets, without sheets. We carried canned goods, sea biscuit, coffee, eggs, tea, canned milk. A pack of cards and a cribbage board.

The Captain stood on the shore of the Sheepscot while we shoved off, with an old gunny sack around his shoulders, for a fine mist was coming in. When the *Josy* stuck on a nest of reeds, he rushed into the water to give her a push, his old shoes, with the leather slashed to accommodate his bunions, quacking. "She'll pick up a breeze once you hit the channel," he shouted, for we had suddenly caught the current and were moving out. Then he climbed the bank and stood waving. He grew smaller; he stopped waving. Lifting a hand, he held it open-palmed toward us. Then he dropped the hand, to trudge up the hill, but paused, turned, lifted one hand once more, shyly, shoulder high, keeping it steady as he might have held a lighted lantern. The island came between, and we lost him.

We never did get to New York. We hit squalls, were becalmed on a steamy open sea without a breeze in sight; then squeezed into Porpoise Harbor before a hurricane broke, and jigged around for two days in company with sardine fishermen and big yachts from Bar Harbor, crouched in our tiny cabin, playing cribbage or heating canned beans over the Sterno. When the sun broke, the third day, we were the second boat out of the harbor. The first was a sardine-fishing boat, whose crew tossed us a rope so we could get out the narrow mouth under their power. The seas were running high, but she went out like a bird. The crews on the big yachts were just beginning to stir on deck. When they saw us flying out over the shiny water, they gave us a big salute. That little ketch was a beautiful sight! Big yachts would alter their course to come up beside her to ask what make she was. Some thought her no less than an aristocratic Alden ketch, she was so dainty, so shipshape, so well made with her shiny black hull, her white cabin with little portholes, her beautiful red-and-white sails.

We got her as far as Cohasset, near the Cape Cod Canal, before we beached her. We had to. It had taken three weeks to get her that far, and our money was running out. We hated to leave her, loyal as she was and high-spirited as a horse. But in some ways we were eager to be quit of her. One may love reality better, sometimes, after a long detour by way of dreams, and now that more than summer had ended, we wanted to be free of her. The day we decided not to make the run to New York but to try and get her to the other side of Boston was marked in a way we couldn't ignore. For it was the day we sailed through a thick fog across Casco Bay to Portland and very nearly didn't make it. Sacco and Vanzetti didn't make it; on that same day, after the stroke of midnight, they were executed.

If we hadn't wanted to get to Portland that night, we might not have tried to sail in so thick a fog. But we wanted to be where we could hear the news. For some reason we half expected a last-minute miracle. At eight in the morning the fog was so thick you couldn't see the dock in the little harbor where we had spent the night. But at nine it began slowly to lift, and we sculled out of the harbor to make the first lap around the buoys. The Coastal Guide warned that it was a tricky passage in any weather, filled with shoals and hidden reefs, sudden islands and mysterious currents. We laid the chart out on the cabin; wiped off the gluey mist from the compass. Because it was so calm, I was more at ease than I had a right to be. Out of pure ignorance. On other days, in the deep trough of an iron wave, I had been sick with fear, petrified in the cabin, where stretched out on a bunk I would expect to be plunged to the bottom in the black coffin of the *Josy*. John, of course, was an expert swimmer. I could not swim, but neither could the old Captain. I could never get into my head that to a true skipper the sound of breakers is a signal of dread. To me it intimated blessed land.

As the sails were so languid, barely moving, the breeze so light, we tacked back and forth with the patience of a spider stitching a fine web. The lazy needlelike movement sometimes lulled me to sleep, but only for a moment. Waking was always the same. You were inside some vast cocoon, and it was sticky with a wetness that soaked the skin. It clung to your hair like damp bees. We might have been alone, except for the sound of the foghorns mooing in the distance of watery pastures. But the fog warped the view of immediate objects; the masts soared to twice their size, to be caught in the swathing vapors; as in one of the crazy mirrors at Coney Island, John's six-foot stature elongated to a giant's. Sitting calmly, in the red cotton jacket of a Breton fisherman, his hand on the tiller, he held his head alert as a bird's, listening. Once we came about fast at the sound of breakers and, edging off, saw the fanged tusks of a great slimy rock loom green to port. But mostly we sat listening with the rapt attention of devoted music lovers at Carnegie Hall to an unseen choir: the ponderous chugging of an invisible steamer, the moan of the bell buoys, the piercing spectral whistle off Cape Elizabeth. By identifying the sounds, we could mark the stages of our passage. Once a motorboat sheered past us out of the fog. A man with a long pole stood upright as a gondolier in the prow, feeling in the water ahead as a blind man might use his cane. Startled at the sight of us, they veered sharply and, lifting a hand in a silent salute, passed rapidly as an apparition.

At five o'clock we were still moving through the white visceral matter of some monster sheep's brain. We had eaten our dry peanut butter sandwiches; drunk our thermos of coffee; smoked cigarettes. The coils of fog took on a violet pallor; a gull suddenly broke through, to zoom over us. Then a sudden roar of warning breakers forced us about fast. The rudder skidded on the water, flopped, and snagged on the butt of the hull. The pin had twirled heavily to the bottom. John lifted the rudder out and flung it in the cockpit. "Take the tiller out," he said. "I'll have to steer now with the oar."

"Are we going to make it?"

"I don't know," he said. "With a breeze no bigger than your hand, we must have been drifting. I've tried to allow for it. We may be heading straight into port. We may be heading out to sea, past Cape Elizabeth. If we are, there will be nothing to do but ride it out all night. If we don't get a blow, it's all right."

But at six o'clock the light changed suddenly, as though someone had lighted up a room back of a curtain. "The sun must be shining somewhere," John said. "And look, there's a bunch of gulls riding." The next second, straight ahead of us, the fog rolled up as slowly and steadily as a curtain in a theater, and there were the roofs and houses, the ribbons of streets of a town glittering in pure sunlight: Portland!

We moored the *Josy* in the harbor. It was like putting a faithful horse into its stall. Took down her sails, locked the cabin, got in the dinghy, rowed ashore, tied up the dinghy. Too tired to think of sleeping aboard, we hunted up an old hotel, where they gave us an enormous room with two narrow beds stranded in the watery blue waste of a worn carpet. We ate spaghetti in a dockside EAT joint. Two soiled-jacketed stewards off a boat were shaking dice at the end of the counter. The counterman was a stout Italian in a clean white apron. When I complimented him on his spaghetti and asked if he ever made it with butter and garlic sauce, his face lighted up, and leaning on the counter, he confided, "You like it? No call for garlic sauce. Meat they want, ham and eggs," and, shrugging, turned up a tiny radio a bit higher. Sports news was coming through. A voice said that fog was heavily blanketing the entire New England coast. A sardine-fishing boat had been rammed by a freighter. The Coast Guard had rescued several small craft.

We went outside and walked around. Waiting. The fog was coming in again, in huge puffs like smoke. One minute you could see to the corner, the next, no farther than a foot away. We pushed open the door of a drugstore, hunting postcards; wrote one to the Captain. "It was like going into the eye of a needle to make it," John wrote, adding, "She's a good little ship." I added, "He's a good captain, or we wouldn't have made it."

There were several hours to go. We felt our way through the fog to the harbor, located the dinghy, but the *Josy* was hidden from sight. "I hope her anchor holds and it doesn't blow," John said. Then, "I suppose we should have gone to Boston. Not that it would have done any good." There wasn't much we wanted to talk about, but the way people do who are waiting together in a house where someone is sick unto death, we wanted to say something. "I never expected anything from Coolidge," John said. "Nor from the governor. Nor all the rest. Except Brandeis and Holmes. I never will understand why they did what they did." His voice held the hurt of a son who has been betrayed by a father.

"There's never anyplace to sit down in America," I complained.

"You aren't supposed to sit. You're supposed to be up and doing."

"You remember how Sacco said, 'Kill me or set me free'?" I said.

"I guess they'll kill him, all right," John said. "They seem to think they have to purify the city with a sacrifice. Like in old Athens, where they led out two of the most debased citizens: as an offscouring, they called it. To get rid of a pestilence or a famine. What was it they called them? *Pharmakos*. First they gave them cheese and a barley cake. Then they beat them with branches from the wild fig tree, then they burned them. Scattered the ashes into the sea and to the winds as a general cleanup. That's the way they did it."

"You think we are any smarter?"

Once we visited our hotel room. It was a gloomy vault. Once we stopped in front of a ship chandler's shop, rubbed the mist from the window, and peered in at the fascinating array of ropes, bobbins, compasses, barometers, hardy utensils for Shipmate stoves, heavy boots, slickers, fishing nets, and life jackets.

"Let's go back to the Italian's," John said. "He had a

good face." We climbed on stools. The Italian gave a pleased little sign of recognition. Two truckdrivers were noisily arguing over ham and eggs. We drank our coffee hastily from the thick cups. The radio signaled midnight. The truckdrivers, still arguing, threw down their money and left without shutting the door. John got up to close it. Now the voice came on. The prison would have to go dark, the lights out, to kill them. It went dark. Then lights on again. Then dark again. The Italian had been standing still as a statue. Now he took off his apron and hung it on a peg. Rolled down his sleeves over strong thick-muscled hairy arms. He reached up to turn out a light, hesitated, his hand still on the switch, looking at us. We were sitting quiet, without saying anything. It was time to go. Then he looked around in a swift running glance, as if he might be overheard, and softly, as if he were on tiptoe, came to the counter and leaned heavily on it, looking me straight in the eyes. His face was tense but calm; one of his eyebrows was nicked with a scar. He spoke in a quiet voice, confidentially. "Electricity. Is that what it's for? Is that the thing to do? Seven years they waited. Not bad men. No. *Good* men."

We must have said something. But what, I can't remember. All that I knew was that a conclusive event had happened. What it meant I couldn't have defined. Looking back from this distance, I might add explanations that would signify. But I don't want to do that. I want to try to keep it the way it was, back there, on the early morning of August 23, 1927, when we walked out on the foggy streets, feeling very cold in our sweaters, and reached out to take one another's hand for the walk back to the hotel. Without saying a word, we both felt it and knew that we felt it: a kind of shuddering premonition of a world to come. But what it was to be we could never have foreseen. Not the density of fog, the bewildering calls from deceptive buoys, the friends lost in the mist, the channels marked for death. The port harder to find than the eye of any needle.

We were tender with one another when we came to our damp room. John punched the beds. "This one isn't so hard. You take it," he said.

"No," I said. "I don't want to take it. You did the work today. You take it." In the night, I woke to find him standing at the long window. A dog was barking. "What's wrong?" I called to him, getting out of bed.

"We're drifting," he answered. "Hear that dog? We're drifting on the rocks. The anchor must be dragging." The fog swirling through the open window made the room a ship at sea.

"No," I said. "We're not on the boat. We're in the hotel. Come to bed."

So far as I am concerned, what had been the twenties ended that night. We would try to penetrate the fogs to come, to listen to the buoys, to read the charts. It would be three years before we took down a volume of *Kunstgeschichte* from our shelves, to be replaced by a thin narrow book in red entitled *What Is to Be Done?*, by V. I. Lenin. Then in a few years it would be taken down to be replaced by another. And so on.

How could I have known that night in Portland that once we had beached the *Josy* at Cohasset I would never see her again? But I never did. Years later John went to look for her, alone, and found her bashed in by a heavy tide, the planks rotted, her skeleton white as bone. He wrote me about it. For by that time we had parted, and I no longer saw him.

Yesterday's Road

*I*N 1943, when I was in Washington on the German desk of our war propaganda agency, I was interrogated by two Investigators, who asked, among other questions, why I had gone to the Soviet Union in 1930. The commonsense answer would have been "Why not?" but common sense always looks treasonable in wartime.

The Interrogators were an Irish Catholic and a Jew: middle-aged nice family men who were only doing a job. They had nothing to do with the procedure that required each charge to be introduced with a curious wording, such as, "It is Reported that in 1930 you went to the Soviet Union." There were a good many of these charges, linked to the events of the thirties and the role I had played in connection with each, and given them in bulk, I was impressed by the record.

In that big, impersonal room with its clean tables, shiny chairs, and vacant windows opening on a wispy sky, the voices of the men, in ritualistic devotion to the recurring phrase *It is Reported,* began to sound like an incantation and to cast a spell. The scenes that flashed to my mind's eye were more vivid than the factual line of the wording, which meant less than the subtitles on a Charlie Chaplin silent movie, where that anarchic and immortal lily of the field, the tramp, gives a backward kick at the impassive form of a slow-witted policeman before he flatfoots it around the corner and wings his way beyond. I might say that in the whirlwind of events, doors had slammed. The vagabond road to the twenties was blocked. The inquiring journeys of the thirties, made for evidence, not for "kicks," had ended in this office.

In a pinch you may remember the wildest scenes, blown up like dust from a distant explosion. As I remembered *Nach Paris* scrawled in chalk on the German boxcars, which I had seen only in photographs in Berlin, the jubilant *Soldaten* of the First World War Wehrmacht jamming the doorways on their way toward Paris. But their *Nach Paris* had metamorphosed into our Versailles, and our Versailles into their Berchtesgaden, and Berchtesgaden into a new world war. And thus I was in Washington.

Should I call up, from the debris of the twenties, Rilke's impassioned line "Choose to be changed. With the flame be enraptured!" Too literary for the present customers. But it had ignited the flambeau of the thirties, "Change the world," and no doubt about it, the world had changed. So had I. Should I try to go back to the crossroads where my own history intersected the history of our time? But every crossroads is a split diamond. And what would it get me? The real events that influence our lives don't announce themselves with brass trumpets but come in softly, on the feet of doves. We don't think in headlines; it's the irrelevant detail that dreams out the plot. You may have to go back to the blue bowl that held your infant bread and milk; or watch the sun shoot a dazzling arrow along the white tablecloth.

Or listen for the squawk of the alarmed goose that once rode in a basket on the hard seat of a German third-class train. Or replay the scene where the doughboys gleefully sang, "How ya gonna keep 'em down on the farm, after they've seen Paree?" Before they went back to the farm to burn wheat in the thirties, to sell corn for a nickel a bushel, and to defy, with a dangling rope, the sheriff who came to foreclose the old homestead.

I had been fired, abruptly, without being told the reasons why and at a moment when I was due to be promoted to the New York office or overseas. Though this particular inquiry was to end with the approval of my qualifications by the Investigators, they now began to look more like auditors who tally up the assets and liabilities of the alleged bankrupt before writing him off. I had the right of appeal, but I no longer wanted the post, which now seemed to designate me more as a spook in a war poster than as an actor in a spectacular and moving pageant. What's more, I had no money to linger on in Washington to petition, to hang around in corridors and "present my case." Nor was I convinced that the paper bullets our outfit was firing over the airways could have any effect.

In those early days, we were of course only tuning up, with a lot of raw recruits from the sticks as well as slick adepts from New York. My colleague on the German desk was a splendid young history specialist, trained at Princeton, and we both kept asking: Whom are we aiming at? The Nazis? The old Social Democrats? The Communists? The Junkers? Or that inchoate putty mass, which can be pushed around and exists everywhere and nowhere? For if you hope to bend minds to a purpose, you must know to whom and to what you speak. We prodded, until one day we were summoned to an office and given a chunk of thick typed "directives" to read, with the solemn proviso that we were to make no notes and must keep every comma incommunicado. A secretary was present as we sat sedately, and it was my mistake to laugh. Not that it mattered; I would have been fired anyhow. But who could help it? Even my more discreet colleague smothered a twitching mouth to mutter, "Quiet. There's a war on."

The directives, presumed to be of deep psychological import, were mostly for *Hausfrauen* into whose unwilling ears we were to pour demoralizing suspicions concerning their absentee husbands. For wives with men on the western front: Remember, not the French *poilu*—who had already officially capitulated—but the artful French sirens. Could a German housewife expect her man, on his return, ever to be quite the same again? Toward the east, the danger was equally insidious. Their women, too, might transform a potent warrior into a sexual malingerer. But there were also paper bullets for the fighting men, who were to be twitched by their erotic roots and reminded that their home fire pullulated. Beware the horde of war prisoners and displaced persons—foreign types leaking in through crevices, who might be useful on the home front to spade the wife's garden, to plow, to feed the pigs, but many of whom were strong physical specimens. Could a woman's honor prevail over stark loneliness, dark winters, frost, the cries of the flesh? Did they want to come back from the gory front to find a stranger's chick hatched in their nest?

As propaganda, the directives struck me as about as effective as a loaf of our cottony bread. I knew a good deal about Germany, though not enough: I had lived there for two years in the twenties, had returned in 1930 and again in 1935 for the *New York Post*. I had learned something about actual war, that guns and bombs crushed more than a dozen eggs, when I was in Madrid in 1937 while the city was daily bombarded. As a woman, I felt a certain conceit in my awareness of the violent potentials simmering within situations and human beings. This stuff was silly. Hunger would have made more sense: older Germans remembered its pangs from the First World War; younger ones from the rickety legs of kids during the inflation. But *sex*—if I knew what I was talking about, damaged goods would have more appeal than empty arms, and the women knew it, the men knew it, and would be more likely to laugh than to weep at our piety. *Sex*—to *Germans,* who were pulverizing Jews and politicals by the million!

I could remember some quoted lines from an old notebook where it was said that each man, according to his racial and social milieu and to the specific point in his individual evolution, is a kind of keyboard on which the external world plays in a certain way. All keyboards have an equal right to exist. All are equally justified. Something of the kind had even been built into our own Bill of Rights. But now these words sounded hollow, echoes from a departed summer twilight when the wooden croquet balls had jovially knocked against one another on the green lawn. In the convulsed knock of world upon world, could an individual keyboard hope to sound a single, clear, personal, or harplike note? In war, a mechanical master keyboard takes over, like some monster player piano, to drown out the piping of solitary and singular instruments.

The two Investigators and I might add up a column of facts and *It is Reported*s without agreeing on the final sum. Nor did childhood memories count; they might hopelessly entangle. The two of them had doubtless saluted our flag in local grade schools, as I had in Iowa when a militant principal tapped her little bell like a drum major; on Washington's birthday she marshaled the troop of pupils in a body to the main hall, where the drum rolled, a trumpet bugled, and the beautiful flag was unfurled. We stood, rows of impression-able infants, to chant in unison, "I pledge my heart [hand on heart, ready to be broken] and my hand [outstretched hand, ready to be blown off] to my country." One Country, One Nation, Indivisible, and One Flag. Drums. Star-Span-gled Banner. Shivery, exalted, my voice rang out. Did we also promise our heads? Not as I recollect it. I had my own fable, and fables speak.

But if the headpiece was inviolable, could it be granted immunity from the flesh? No head versus heart, mind versus flesh, here. Words, too, are carnal. My own *doppelgänger* might split an apple with me, take the core and give me the fruit, but more often it spoke in riddles. Or hinted that immersion in the vital present, an immersion, alas, achieved by an uncritical acceptance of the drift of things, could defeat the aims of any goal. Ready and intoxicating spon-taneity had its price. I could feel the pinch of it in that office, and if I seem to be putting on bland airs now, from an experienced distance, I was becoming sick at heart at the time. As often as I had rehearsed risky situations, dramatiz-ing myself in major, important roles, I had neglected this smaller domestic opening for a minor part. I wasn't in a maniac Gestapo cellar, nor confronted by a merciless judge in a Moscow trial. The sadism of the parlor and gallery that the Surrealists had deliberately cultivated as a proof of their power to shock, and to delight, had passed over and beyond any of Max Ernst's bestiaries of animals with human heads, which now looked like benign beings compared with the factual evidence of the "real" world. But we were no police state, though it seemed we had engaged its footboys. The very politeness of my Interlocutors unhinged me, made me regard trivialities with concern. I noted with alarm one ink-stained finger of my gloves; another finger was ripped. A bit more of this, and I would begin to simper, "Shall I pour the tea?"

Moments like this can relegate you to a dungeon, with nothing to contemplate except your own abyss. I had no intention of retreating to the thirteenth century or to the fascinating eighteenth. Nor of calling on Pascal, Plato, or Thucydides, to the extinction, for instance, of Rosa Luxemburg, Madame Rolland, or Danton. Nor of apologizing or stuttering away my birthright or ceding to strangers the ground rights to my own experience, my own mistakes. Or even to my own ignorance. To do so would close the debate. What I understood very well was that the dry rattle of all these *It is Reported*s might be calculated to reduce some of my best yesterdays to outworn slogans; telephone numbers of people who were no longer there, or were dead; and foxed files.

They could take *It is Reported that in Madrid, in 1937, you broadcast in behalf of the Spanish Loyalists,* turn it inside out, and find me involved in a conspiracy, where I saw only evidence of my own well-grounded reasons of the heart. Or what was I to make of the Report that I had signed a petition in 1932 protesting the violation of civil liberties in Detroit? No details were given, and I couldn't remember what it had been all about. Or the one on the piece for the *New Masses* in 1935, when Batista was shooting students on the university steps, while in the mountains near Santiago peasants stood with machetes, behind virgin trees, to guard their land and what they took to be their rights from soldiers who were mounting the slopes in obedience to commands from the sugar planters in the valley below. I no longer wrote for the *New Masses,* nor would, nor *could.* But it had served my keyboard once, as my piece had doubtless served theirs. And I stood by the substance of it, which had its own life and veracity apart from either author or publication. I had only to remember the frail wishbone from a skinny chicken the mountain folk had shared with me, which a child, who had never gone to school, had pressed into my hand at parting.

So I said, "Why do you keep saying, *It is Reported*, when it is a fact?" But what is a *fact?* Who is to interpret it? What ideas ride on its back? And a protean Me wanted to break the cords that bind, and to soar, if only back to my attic, where there was some hope of getting to the source of things. If the truth about Me was what was wanted, they might better scrabble in the old gladstone bag, near the window where the squirrel got in. Nothing within except a bunch of love letters, some tied together with a ribbon, others with a string or a busted rubber band; or in ink, or pencil, or typed; addressed to Madam, Mme., Mlle., Fräulein, Señorita, Mrs., or Miss. One clawed with a stern warning: *Destroy.*

Or they could fumble on the shelf where old newspapers were stacked, and where they might lay hands on copies of old little magazines such as *The Little Review*, which I had carried to classes at Berkeley in 1917 instead of a ball of wool to knit a sock for a soldier boy; or the number that was banned when the editors printed a section of *Ulysses*. Or find *The Masses* before its editors were indicted for treasonable intent in opposing the Great War and the magazine was suppressed. Whatever happened to the seventy-year-old scholar with a shock of beautiful white hair, in a house in Berkeley, who had explained with enthusiasm what he believed to be the meaning of the Bolshevik takeover? Did he change his mind or, like Victor Serge, stick with the Old Guard? They might stumble over a box of photographs, to

find a glum Hemingway in a stocking cap, with rod and
reel. What could they make of Katherine Anne Porter, arms
akimbo, posed with a rakish John Herrmann as a song-and-
dance vaudeville team? I knew what they'd think of the jolly
German soldiers in Madrid, lolling on the grass, who signed
their first names on the back, but not their last. Or that one
of Nathanael West and me as worthy old peasants on a
wintry day, huddled in chilly coats: on his head, a sloppy
hunter's hat; on mine, a shawl. While we brazenly held aloft
a hammer and a sickle: he, the hammer; I, the sickle.
Crossed, as duelists had once crossed swords. Or damning
evidence: a photograph of me taken in Moscow, 1930. Por-
trait of the Author in a round cap, three-quarter view;
eyelashes sloping downward over serious, downcast eyes;
hand on table, open like an open book; expression watchful,
listening, tender, and intense.

Were these courteous gents the hosts, or were they my
guests? It was nearing the cocktail hour. Why not take the
deadweight out of facts and hand them a taste of mortal life?
So I volunteered that they'd forgotten a thing or two, such
as the day in Paris in 1935 when I had come out of Germany
and had stood on the sidelines of the great funeral procession for Henri Barbusse. His body rode on a caisson, as it
deserved to ride, for he had fought as a private in the First
World War and had written his antiwar novel, *Le Feu*, after
he was demobilized. It had enlightened my green youth
before our country came in as an ally. And that procession
had been notable for me, not for its pomp, for it had none,
but for the delegations from dozens of small towns, marching by the hundreds in formations of blue working-clothed
ranks and bearing homemade wreaths; and for the huge
glass hearses, of the old-fashioned, ornate type, that were
loaded within and without with great bouquets of wilting

field flowers—blue cornflowers, red poppies, clover—and sheaves of golden wheat, which had been brought to the funeral train as it passed through Poland, Germany, and France on its way out of Moscow, where Barbusse had died; and for the construction workers standing as silent witnesses on the scaffoldings at the tops of buildings, and the women and children crowded in windows along the miles where the procession passed on its way to Père Lachaise.

And among this throng had marched a band of exiles from Germany: poor, dismantled, and conspicuous for the absurd precision of their disciplined marching among the more loosely jointed, more happily assembled French. Had their discipline been of use only to make martyrs? Or to divide themselves? For some of the marchers were to show up in Spain in the International Brigade in 1937, claiming that if you wanted to see Berlin, go to Madrid. Nor had they foreseen in Madrid the fratricidal divisions to follow, or that concentration camps would await them in France after defeat, or death in the Moscow purges, or that they would flee to Mexico, Rio, or Buenos Aires, and some be denied America; or that some, brother against brother, might find themselves once more secretly at dagger's point with one another but fighting together with the Resistance in Europe.

The two men listened—gentle, clerklike—and then let me go, toting up the figures to clear the bill of lading. Was their favorable verdict made out of pique against their rival investigators who had stolen their priority? I could not know, or care: the job was gone. I did not fancy that without me the war might be lost. I was as certain we would win as I had been that Hitler would not last his thousand years, nor the Russians crumple in two weeks as the Nazi tanks moved eastward. Not that I prided myself on superior diagnostic powers: of such I had none. Often I had miscalculated and misfired; often engaged in internal combat while in combat without. One Me, a jaundiced eye on Progress, was a gloomy prognostician; the other, a congenital cricket, ready to chirp, "While there's life, there's hope." No, what most struck me was that my Interlocutors and I spoke the same tongue but lacked the elements of a common language. On my native soil, I was in a kind of no-man's-land, more strange than I had been when first I went to Germany and loved to drift anonymously with the crowd. And just as I fancied then that because I could glibly read *Faust* in German I might hear and speak of Germany, so I had come to this outfit plumed with formal qualifications but unhanded by secret laws at cross-purposes with my own.

To blend our differences I would have had to sink myself in their total life, as once I had dissolved among Germans in the inflation days of 1923: when I had mingled with the rich in swank hotels and spas; or nibbled ersatz cakes with uneasy bourgeoisie in a pleasant pension on Kastanienallee while they regaled me with reports of outmoded delicacies, dishes now moribund: a dozen eggs, a pint of cream, split almonds, a fistful of Orient spices, which took shape before their eyes, then exploded to their hysterical wonderment; or shared black bread and cabbage with students in their unheated *Studentenheim* in Marburg, where a youthful Pasternak had once climbed the steep cobbled streets; or paid ten cents to take a train to Dresden to hear the opera, to look upon that Raphael Madonna that Dostoevsky once complained had overenraptured Turgenev; or reveled each night at a different theater, where needy Germans strained to spend their marks before tomorrow made them trash, and thronged for Ibsen, Strindberg, and Shakespeare, and for their own playwrights, who in fabulous stage

III

settings set on fire the follies of their age, their bedevilment, their savaged predicament.

Or copied in my notebook, with a novitiate's pride, sage sayings. George Kaiser, *Berliner Tageblatt,* Sept. 4, 1923, on the poet as creator of the only history meaningful to man: "He orders the confusion. He draws the line through the hubbub. He constructs the law. He holds the filter. He justifies man." Or noted Werfel, hailing man as the name-giver, the one who expresses the unexpressed, lifts the world out of the unconscious and thus creates once more the cosmos. *Erkenntnis,* intellectual insight, was Heinrich Mann's motto; he claimed space for intellectual man to remake the social world according to the ideals of justice and reason. Shy and reticent, I circled around that circle about Herwarth Walden and his *Der Sturm,* where poets shucked off burdensome syntax, shed *Gemût,* elevated the noun and verb to do their work of reshaping and reseeing, and brought the arrow of their desire to its mark, shorn of all circumlocution, description, diffuseness. And I was drowned in awesome reverence for the new, and then drew back in fright; read Gottfried Benn's poem "Happy Youth," in which a drowned girl's body serves as a nest for a brood of rats—the Happy Youth are rats, not men. And saw its constructs reveal an icy vision of total indifferences to human woe and universal death, where devouring rats could frolic—and nonmen.

And then? I don't know why I forsook this intoxicating realm, but there were echoes from the very paving stones, sounds in the air and black birds in the sky, and I dived down and for months lived cheek by jowl with the poor in gloomy tenements of Moabit and Wedding. And you can say that the poor won; and that I came out of Germany, in 1924, pro-German, for whatever that implies for those days.

Nor could the dazzle of Paris; the rich, heady air; or falling in love; or idling along the quay with a modest, happy Hemingway; or calling hello to a ruddy-bearded Pound—none of this could wipe away that vital, decisive stain, which blended deep and harsh and took its toll in years to come. What could my Interlocutors understand of this? The experience was my own; no outsider could subtract it from my totality. Who is to rob you except yourself? The heart must weigh the stone it earns.

By 1930 the road had lengthened out to reach to Moscow. Our government did not recognize the Soviet Union, no more than China now, but we could go to a writers' conference there provided the Russians approved our visas. John Herrmann and I sailed on the *Bremen*. We went third class, where there was no promenade deck, only a small space, about twelve feet by six, jutting out close to the water at the stern. This space was always packed with silent, intent men—looking back. "Third cabin" was a modern equivalent of the old-time steerage and now held many immigrants who were sad to return, pushed out by the crunch of rising joblessness and by the crackdown, too, on all those who held views contrary to the Plan now engineered in the White House by the man who was to tell us, year by year, that Prosperity was just around the corner and would soon appear.

We landed in Bremen and had to wait several days in Berlin, living cheap, hoarding the money we had raised, partly from selling books—a first edition of *Ulysses*, six of the early Paris copies of Hemingway's stories. Then, on a late October at six P.M., John and I stood, two posts, in a great train shed, while round about a crowd of Muscovites churned from up a flight of steps without, past us to their waiting trains. We tried to stop one, then another, but we had no speech they understood, until one man stopped in his tracks and moved back to tap on a pane of glass concealed by hurrying figures within the shabby waiting room.

Out popped a tall woman wearing a once elegant suit of English tweed; her fair hair was knotted in a heavy bun, and she came up to us to ask in English with a Russian accent what she could do for us. We showed her the address of the magazine to which we had been told to go first; she took us to the street, called a droshky driver, and gave him the address; told us how much to pay him and no more; and away we went, clattering over cobbled streets, up high on a teetering back seat, while lower down the driver hunched in a heavy patched coat a foot thick and shouted to his horse, whose fat sides were warmed by his native shaggy barklike covering.

And so we rode on our elevated raft along a street that surged with faces all lifted up to us as we rode, or parted to our vehicle without once breaking the current of their stride. How can I once more gather up the look they gave toward us? Of swift astonishment, deep curiosity, nor stopped a second, but hurried on to catch their trains in the station we had left. The faces are what I remember, bearing down upon us in a thick, pale flood, or upturned to us, as eye met eye. If you've only known an indifferent shopping crowd whose attention drifts toward a show of radios, female finery, or a shiny car, you hardly know how alive a crowd can be, stripped bare of all excrescences; how attentive to the human thing; or how antennae are thrust out, invisibly, from you to them, from them to you, so that like insects in the dark you are drawn toward the scent of the stranger and his curiosity. Their clothes made an odd array:

all shabby, shoes broken down, and some legs wrapped in neat rags or paper; men wore caps, women had dark scarves, the tails hanging down the back like the pigtails of girls. But as to clothes, the Russians all looked more or less alike, male or female: all dun-colored, except for army men, whose uniforms were spick-and-span and could stand up to our best-dressed man. The hollow murmur of many feet, and of our wheels on that street where no shop lights shone, was all the sound there was, except for the crack of our driver's whip and a loud bray from his deep bass voice, shouting something as we passed. It was only later that I found out his bossy shout had been "Make way for the delegation. Make way!"

We halted in a square where dead-eyed buildings stood, and paid our man; got out with our two bags and typewriter; trudged inside the empty corridor. The elevator creaked, and we were the only moving bodies, it seemed; our footfalls echoed as we walked. The door had a name on it; should we knock? We took the American way and boldly flung it open and went in. The room was dim; a long cord dangled a feeble bulb above a group of desks where four men sat. But on our entrance, they all rose up, and like those faces I had once seen on a faraway Montana ranch, where hospitality was a necessity of life not to the travelers alone but to the settlers who pined for outside news, the four showed their suspended eagerness. John had barely said our names, and that we were Americans, when they rushed to us, so it seemed to me, as the old-timers in Russian must have run when they heard the troika bells on the lonely road and welcomed the beginning of felicity. They threw their arms around us; we were kissed. We might have been a heavenly messenger who brings the *panis angelorum*.

Two were Russians: one was Dinamov, the editor of

the *Gazette* and a professor at Moscow University; the other, a robust, dark youth, identified himself as a "specialist" in English and American literature. The other two were Hungarians, one of them ruddy, fierce, with stocky frame; the other, blond and frail, wore a curious rounded hole on his pale cheek, which puckered when he smiled, or showed a glint of bone. He had been lined up against the wall when Hungarian Reds had been trapped in Budapest, and, with a line of brother victims, shot down; they kicked him, but he lay still and waited, and then after dark crawled off through the woods and thus escaped to Russia; and to life, or so he thought.

But who could know what was to come? Not us; we knew so little. The room now buzzed with talk. Yes, our names had been sent in, but who could expect that we might really arrive? People were always promising things that never came to pass. And where to put us? Our new friends hardly knew; the hotels were packed. In a few days, a week, arrangements would be made for guests coming from afar for the conference; and at once, we were pressed to be their guests and to go to Kharkov to meet the writers of the revolutionary vanguard. Someone telephoned; the Critic, as we came to call the specialist on American goods, volunteered that John should stay with him; they had so much to talk about. As for me, they had just the spot, in the apartment of an agronomist who spoke German and came home late at night, to whom I could talk German and tell my needs. So far we had been talking mixtures of English, German, and French, and by touch and look added to the sense.

John left first, and thereafter, for some days, we met only to exchange views or to wander, hand in hand, through the streets. He told how the Critic's "place," described in advance as "commodious," had turned out to be a narrow cell, furnished only with books stacked to the ceiling and a tight bed too short for John's long frame; his feet stuck out. The Critic insisted his guest must take the bed, and he himself lay grandly on the floor, covered by an overcoat. At night a rat pounced out and was squelched when our Critic nonchalantly threw a shoe. But night for sleep was short; the Critic was all aglow with talk and tea; a little vodka too. He was translating Proust, not for general consumption but for the knowing few. He failed to pass the Kafka test but was impressed that we had been fishing with Hemingway in Key West a few months before. Dreiser and John Dos Passos should have come. He loved success. *Ulysses* was too deep, he felt, for present days; the translation problems too austere for him. He must learn the idiom and, on that first night, had insisted we send him samples of *all* our magazines on our return. Especially the *Saturday Evening Post* and the detective story publications.

The huge apartment building where my agronomist had a nook had once been a fancy club for dissolute rich young men and had been gouged out in wedges to accommodate some of the more modest bureaucracy. An elevator landed us on the sixth floor; the door was opened by a girl with a round, chubby face. She wore a kerchief on her fair hair, and a tough apron covered her from top to toe. My escort handed in a parcel, which contained a hunk of precious butter and a jar of caviar for me. I stepped inside, but what to say? Our speech jangled odd sounds, we laughed, and from another room a plump woman sailed out, smiling, accompanied by an older, taller girl, slim and lovely, who asked me if I knew French; she was learning it. She would teach me Russian right away; she was dying to learn English; we could exchange. Right now I must have something to eat. But first, a bath!

They took away my hat, my coat, my bag. There was a big open zinc tub in the room, near the fat kitchen stove, on which pots steamed. The chubby one motioned me to undress, and the mother and her daughter withdrew. I undressed slowly and waited for privacy, but none came. The chubby one stood adamant; I was to get into the tub. I did, and knelt while she poured from a big tin pitcher a stream of warm water upon my head and me. I hadn't wanted my long hair washed, but washed it had to be. There was a tiny sliver of soap I feared would melt away, but it did not. I got out, there was a hot towel waiting, and I dressed, mounted a few steps from the kitchen to the dining room, where a beaded hanging lamp shone bright above a darned white tablecloth. My butter was set out, black bread, and quantities of jeweled caviar. There was a fried egg, crisp and hot, a pot of tea, and so I began to eat, with a Russian lesson for dessert. A little boy with a thin, eager face joined us, leaning his chin upon the table. The mother worked away, unraveling an old sweater to wind up its wool. My teacher would lift up a knife, say its Russian name; I would repeat, then give the English name; she echoed it, and her little brother pantomimed. Before we parted for the night I knew the names of all the dishes on the table, how to say I would like some tea, thank you and goodbye and how are you, the words for where and what, for hot and cold, how to ask what time is it and what do you call this street.

The room where I was to sleep was choked with an enormous rubber plant, resting against a tubercular window of sickly hue, and two narrow beds. I was to sleep in one; the chubby girl in the other. But the little boy had given up his bed for me; he was to sleep on two chairs pushed together, on which a fat pillow served as mattress, with a thick blanket flung over all. I protested it wasn't right to put him out of his bed; but his mien was proud, he smiled, and in Russian said what may have been "Please, it's nothing." The room went dark, the children fell asleep; the moonlight filtered through the rubbery leaves to make a greenish pool, in which we all three floated, the night through, in our aquarium.

I only saw and talked to the agronomist once, when late at night he sat on a stool in the room beyond the kitchen, at the top of the flight of steps, and looked then like some tired man who has been made to sit too long and may fall asleep before he has finished his bowl of soup. But the second I mounted the steps between, he woke up with a smile to shake my hand and to ask, how did I fare, was there anything he could do? By this time I had nosed around and could have asked a dozen questions but refrained. Would he have told me of the vast collectivization plan then afoot, which would uproot flocks of human beings from their ground, to starve or die? I doubt it. Perhaps he himself was not in on the plan, or what it foreboded. I knew far less, so told him of my youth in Iowa, where they raised corn and pigs and wheat. That was bait for him; he leaped at it, asked me a dozen questions about crops and machines; he had heard our farmers were not doing well.

The hour was late, but in low voices we talked on and on. What was said? I don't remember his words, only that he unwound a drama of a vast and suffering land, with the unnamed protagonist an absent Machine that could do the work of many hands. I was not making judgments but sopping up and taking in; or tutoring my backward keyboard to new tunes. How to reconcile Rimbaud's *la Vraie Vie* with the Commune?

I only know those days were best before the delegations swept in; we could poke around, stare at pictographs in front of empty stores, showing a fish, a loaf, a shoe to illustrate for the illiterate what was sold there once but not now. Or at evening see the empty rooms light up with a lamp, a candle or two, while around a long table heads with caps or hooded with a shawl pored laboriously over a copybook, intent on the key that would release the clue. Or, with an Englishman who spoke Russian and had lived there for months, visit a steel plant, the first I'd ever seen, doubtless the last: factories aren't my style. We moved around, electrified to see a great black bowl tip its scalding contents down, while a giant sheathed in leather wrestled with a huge red-hot snake, which writhed until it was subdued to a long, dark shank for a train to glide upon. And wondered when a little group of men, working at this and that, dropped their tools to follow us about, to press close. I'd ask, "What's he saying?" and they'd ask, was it true that in America every workingman owned his own car? And what did we think of Walt Whitman? How did their steel plant compare with ours? Was Victor Hugo a revolutionary poet—what did we think?

Once, wandering on the dim night streets with the Critic, we stopped to chat with a Russian night owl, who stood with hands in pockets of a jaunty leather jacket and opined that he'd never had it so good or thought to earn so much, except—alas—there was nowhere much to go and nothing much to spend it on. Or we went with one of the Hungarians, as on a spree, to a factory meeting that turned out to be a poetry reading, and saw the intent faces, still as a clear flame, lighted up until the poem ended. One night we dropped into a basement den where the Critic promised other writers were sure to be. Rousing voices rumbled, tea was poured. We were introduced to a saturnine man, hunched in a black leather jacket. He was Leonid Leonov, a good writer, the Critic said, but like others of the older school, he found it difficult to make "the transition." The writer turned, bowed formally, and, with an odd, faint, hostile smile, turned his back.

Where *were* the Russian writers? Did they hide? Some years before Mayakovski had visited New York, had come arrogantly proud, bellicose, youthful, and intent. I had never met him, only felt the contagion of his presence: in an East Side dump he had enthralled a group of ardent youths and then departed, unheralded by the great, known by few.

It was Mayakovski, I had most hoped to meet; now he was dead, six months before: a suicide. But what of Babel or Pasternak? Gorky, too, was present only by his absence. Or what of the jolly pair who had written *The Golden Calf?* Or the ubiquitous Ilya Ehrenburg? Where was Pilnyak? Why was it that when the conference at Kharkov began, the general of the Red Cavalry, Budenny, strode in like a hero, to great acclaim, but not Babel, who had ridden and fought with him? What was the cavalry without its bard, or Pushkin's statue in the square without Onegin?

Then the Germans streamed in, and, as you might know, order ruled. Our nonchalant strolling days were gone. Ludwig Renn, who had dropped his aristocratic *von* to take a name he coined, proved to be an inflexible as well as indefatigable lecturer on the pros and cons. John and I were now together again, in an old hotel, with delegates from twenty-two countries, so they said. But they said so much. The eight-hour day, the five-day week, the full employment as the rule: no beggars, no prostitutes. Museums, schools, nurseries. Under Renn's command, the joy of riding on a streetcar strung with people swarming like bees was lost; he had to relate the history of the streetcar, its present degenerate state, its bright future as a going concern when more workers could be spared to build new cars again. Churches had become nurseries; here, too, we got a lecture on the bad air, which did not signify. A finger pointed at the rosy children, who, in spite of clammy walls, throve; they did. It almost seemed as if the robust kids should be carrying on their backs the tired mothers who fetched them away. Or we were taken to a big communal kitchen where hundreds of workers were fed; tasted the food and found it excellent; but got a lecture on the future plan that was to rescue housewives from kitchen slavery to work in factories of shiny glass, and would restore to communal brotherhood the eating habits of individual man.

The Germans boasted more delegates than anyone else. All were said to have written books that were declared to be "important" or "brilliant." Anna Seghers was there; she might have posed for Dürer, with her brow and hands. She'd written a sensitive novel about some anarchists, called *The Revolt of the Fishermen.* But where was Brecht?

Ernst Glaeser, a guest like us, not a delegate, was described as "a kind of Hemingway." His novel *The Class of 1902* was antiwar; and so was Ludwig Renn's novel *War,* which he proposed to follow up with one called "Peace." But where was the dramatist Ernst Toller, who had been outlawed from his homeland for years? He'd been a leader in the Bavarian Red Revolution, and his plays had drawn great crowds—some to riot, others to applaud.

You would think if pens were mightier than the sword, then war would have ceased. The twenties had been dominated by the theme that heroes were certain to back out; or to be blacked out by the catastrophe. By 1930 a last tide had swept in Hemingway's *A Farewell to Arms* and Robert Graves's *Goodbye to All That.*

But when the thirties came, Goodbye was turning to Hello, I'm here again. You realized in Moscow, and even more in Kharkov, that war was to be back on the track. It was as plain to see in Berlin or Rome as the sword that Ludwig Renn buckled on the night he made a speech; he had won it as a high-ranking officer in the Kaiser's Wehrmacht. Some held to a private view out of pride or indecision; some of the rich, loathing the wall-to-wall-carpeted minds of their kind, moved sharply to the left; a few, who had the savor of the infinite in their mouths, wanted to see the worst of things and hoped for the apocalypse. Violence had so detonated since the Great War that no one could be quiet anymore. Some took it all in stride; volunteered, so they said, for the duration, in the ranks of the social revolution.

We all bounced off to Kharkov in a train, with Ludwig Renn as a sort of paterfamilias to our car. The official delegation from the States had come: three ultraserious young men whom we had never met before and who looked us up and down as if to say, How did *you* get in the door? But neither did they think much of Mike Gold, the leader of their group, when he blew in solo at Kharkov. The fact was that the Russians loved Mike for his warm, breezy personality, and showed it. They also liked us. But it seemed to me the Faithful Three got little credit for their fidelity. Outside of official recognition and the satisfaction of chores done, they seemed to have little fun. Parties that went on late at night with champagne, vodka, and caviar did not boast their presence. Nor did they approve of the sophisticated French, who brought a worldly gaiety, or of Louis Aragon and his Russian-born wife, Elsa Triolet.

Now, don't expect me to relate all the pros and cons of the debates that went on. It's all been done before. Nor was I one who having sat on a park bench reading Marx was to be rewarded by a sudden illumination. I had never read *Das Kapital* but came to explore other works, both Engels and Rosa Luxemburg, and to deplore that time was short and I had a great background to fill in. But platform speaking never gave me much; I need books and quietude. And the platform talk was barbarous as it trickled in translations. There were some sentences that rang out, bright and sharp, as when a handsome woman—from the Comintern, it was said—got on the platform and, looking down, seemed to direct her talk to me and John and Aragon, and to reprove some of the talk that had brayed for workers' correspondence as the substitute for literature.

There was no time in this era of great depressions or threatened war to write long novels, poetry, or plays, the others had said. What was needed was patient explanation and reports from workers about their toiling lives; what was required were stories of their struggles and their aim; thus building the literature of the new class with the new man. When one of the gloomy Three from the U.S.A. got on the platform to orate, he added his bit to the harangue, scolding that there was no time, no time; that what was needed was plain talk—works like one already printed in the States showing the life and death of a heroic worker.

I was trying to pay attention, to be serious, but at his words, and quite spontaneously, I got up and pushed past knees to leave the auditorium. In a drafty hall, I smoked a cigarette. Aragon came after me, took my arm, and said, "We all know what your position is. You mustn't mind that kind of talk. It's a kind of infantile disease and will wear out." I said, "But it's so funny. Don't you see, the speaker is the author of the very work he extols anonymously."

But when the handsome woman from the Comintern looked down at us, she seemed to understand the more that was at stake. She reminded the stubborn group, who sat stiff-faced, that the great revolutionaries who had brought October to triumph had come from bourgeois strains. That when the proletariat won its goal there would be no bourgeois class, only a classless world, but that in Russia the workers had as yet barely had time to learn to read and write. That the favorite author of Marx had been Balzac. By the time the workers had mastered the world they were to make, what would the term proletariat mean?

The words struck. They might have come from the outlaw Trotsky, whose brilliant book on literature and revolution I had read, as I was to read his *History* after Max Eastman had translated it. But why was it, in reports written by the Faithful and printed back home, I never once heard mention of that speech or her name? Nor, for that matter, was Aragon's name ever brought to the fore or given the aplomb that would have added to the cause. I'll never know; there's too much I'll never know. But knew enough then not to try to write about what I had seen, except for one small piece for the *New Republic,* reporting the conference in capsule.

What the Faithful wrote you can't call lies; they thought it truth. That's the way ideas take root. Their keyboards were struck by winds I could not feel or respond to; dogma to them was the needed arm, not anathema. But one thing sure is that the whole affair told me to beware, beware! Don't get me wrong. In those early years I went as far left as you can go. But I was wary of the chatter, no matter by whom. (I steered clear of our New York political elite, as much as I could, because they knew it all.) I thought, Something overwhelming is at stake, but what? I can't find out here.

We had never before met Aragon. We had some mutual friends, who had described his "white-toothed" smile, his "Roman nose." But what are mutual friends compared with a mutual climate of the mind, a rebel's idealism? Still our keyboards hardly chimed; at least not his and mine. You might say he was of the Paris school and I of Berlin. The Dadaists of the Café Voltaire had split into two camps, one to Paris, one to Berlin; one to become, in Berlin's terms, aesthetes; the other, in Paris's terms, political. So I, too, had been bent more toward the Berlin position, like the Dadaist who had said he needed only to take a single look at the starved and maimed hordes of Berlin to discard his Byronic cravat. The ironic thing was that the Berliners had shed their earlier coats before the Paris Dadaists, now turned Surrealists, took up the political role as 1930 rolled in.

Perhaps the Paris crowd had had their fill; had tired of wandering Paris streets, courting chance: the vertigo of the Unknown. Only vaguely aware of the great industrial strikes that paralyzed their country's economic life, they had wanted freedom; but the free man, as they conceived him, was not so much a man among the living as a dark angel—experimenting, destroying—from whose ideal point of view all human ends pale into pure gratuity. The role of the terrorist, the spy, the saboteur, the traitor, had become transformed. They had named Saint Just the Divine Executioner.

But who of our literary generation was not a Crime Snob of a sort? Who did not lean toward the underdogs, peddlers, thieves, prostitutes, beyond the call of duty: all the underbelly of the world, which looked so fat and smug on top? Perhaps we had gone to Russia because it had been so almost universally despised by the cautious and the respectable. But no surrender to either Nirvana or compulsive obedience.

Who of us had not dreamed of freedom, limpid affections, intensity above all, passionate friendships; and had not become, as well, demanding, possessive? We wanted the universe; we wanted ALL. And leaning out from our traveling trains to wave Farewell, Goodbye, we rounded that long curve, back to war again.

The Starched Blue Sky
of Spain

*A*PART FROM A FEW NEWS ACCOUNTS, a few descriptive articles, I have never written anything about Spain. It had got locked up inside of me. There was one thing you couldn't do when you came back from Spain. You couldn't begin to talk in terms of contradictions. Everyone I knew wanted the authoritative answer. There were characters who had never left New York who were angry with me because I couldn't say for certain that the Trotskyist leader Nin had been murdered. Other characters raged because I refused to accuse Nin of leading a Fascist plot in complicity with Franco. What was wanted was black or white. I wasn't even useful for speechmaking, as I might make a slip and refer to a church where horses were munching hay on the high altar. Religionists might be offended. And by the time I had returned to America the situation had moved to the big courtship phase. To win, everybody had to be wooed. But everybody can't win; and didn't.

If I didn't write, if I didn't speak, it wasn't that I felt ignorant. But it may have seemed to me that what I had brought back was too appallingly diffuse. Like the twigs I used to see the old women in Germany pick up in the forests to tie in little bundles to lug home on their backs. Each twig was precious; it had come from a living tree and would make living fire. I had all sorts of curious oddments: like a pressed flower that grew under a broken olive tree, a bit of quartz from an old cave that had been carved out by the Moors for twenty miles, where families huddled beside little candles during weeks of air raids. I even had a tiny bluish feather that a young Czech soldier had given me one night as we sat by a road in pitchy darkness near the Guadarrama Mountains.

Why do you write a book? Why do you fall in love? Because. It is the one conclusive answer that comes from the bottom of the well. Later you may dress it up with reasons; some of them may very well apply. But *because* is the soundest answer you can give to an imperative. I didn't even want to go to Spain. I had to. Because. It didn't make sense to Max Perkins when I visited him in his office five days before I sailed. He looked at me as one might at a child who had answered the query "Why do you want to run out in the rain and get all wet?" with nothing more than *because.* "What's the matter with all of you?" he asked. "Hemingway's gone off, Dos Passos is there, Martha Gellhorn's going. And now you. Don't you know that Madrid is going to be bombed out? It won't do you any good to go around with the Stars and Stripes pinned on your chests or on your heads. They won't see or care." Now, the unknown is dear to us, and contrary to opinion, security is not the heart's true desire. Death is no deterrent, but its forms may terrify. So for the five nights before I sailed I dreamed of spectacular flames and falling balls of fire in visions never to be rivaled by any reality I was to encounter. As a preview these visions had even a salutary effect. On my first day in Madrid the heavy shelling sounded oddly unconvincing; curiously like one of those torrential thunderstorms we used to get in the Iowa of my childhood.

Don't expect an analysis of events. I couldn't do it then, I can't now. I have my opinions, but what I can only call my convictions go to deeper levels, where opinions hardly count. What's more, those convictions have to do with me, as an individual, and apply to more than events. I can hardly think back upon Spain now without a shiver of awe; it is like remembering how it was to be in an earthquake where the ground splits to caverns, mountains rise in what was a plain. The survivor finds himself straddling a widening crack; he leaps nimbly to some beyond, where he can stand ruminating upon his fate. I suspect that it was the question of my own fate that took me to Spain as much as it was any actual convulsion going on in that country. I certainly didn't run to it as crowds do to a fire. I was respectful and frightened. I had gone through more than one metamorphosis since I was young and had to go to New York. *Because* I had lived for three years in Germany of the twenties—*because*—battening off the ill fortunes of the country, which ordained me a dollar princess with no more to spend than three hundred dollars a year. I had a sprinkling of Spanish, not Castilian but Mexican. Spain was Cervantes and Goya. It took a kind of crust to go to Spain. There was little food in Spain; I would be eating. How was I to pay my way by justifying my presence?

If the pen was even mightier than the sword in a time of crisis, it didn't seem to me that the typewriter held a ghost of a chance against the new weapons. I didn't believe that I could write anything deathless or even sway to any appreciable extent the rigidities that had made for the fantastic nonintervention pact.

Was it possible that I was going in order to live out that early nightmare when as a little girl I read what even Iowa newspapers had carried about the Chicago Iroquois Theatre fire? The element that stuck had been the stampede: the fact that grown men had trampled women and children in their effort to escape. My mother had been horrified by that fact, and almost only that fact: "better to sit quietly in your seat and perish than to have to live the rest of your life with such a memory." For years I could never go to a theater without a secret rehearsal of how I hoped to behave. Nobly, of course. But could anyone be sure? Put to the test, I had more than once proven to be a physical coward; as a child, during two household accidents I had nimbly run from the house and raced around the block, expecting to see the place burst into flames. The sight of blood sickened me, though I took care to let no one know. But the difficulty at finding any root answer to the question of why I or people like me went to Spain is endless. I could just as well claim that the basic reason was that I was a vivid dreamer who had all my life been conscious of the power and art of flying as a peculiarly enviable happiness, and that to soar lightly above trees and over the tops of mountains was a delight so secure that, from early childhood, it had made demands upon actual existence which refused to believe that the impossible might not happen. There *were* miracles; I could testify to it. And there were intimations of possible miracles in Spain.

If I seem to be going into subterranean regions, it is because these regions, as related to myself, are what I know. I don't know anything really about Spain except what came through me and my skin. I believe that my own deeper feelings about myself and the way those feelings attached themselves to the fact of Spain applied to many more than myself. In a certain sense I hoped to find in Spain an antidote to the poison I found in Germany when, in 1935, I went back to a country familiar to me to write a series of articles for the *New York Post* and to try to discover if there was any actual underground movement. The Germany I had known had vanished. Once, traveling on a train to Munich, an old man got into some conversation with me, and on parting said: "Write me a postcard when you get to Paris. I never get any mail anymore. People are afraid to write to one another now." In another sense, I was probably trying to find some answers to the confusions in my own mind. The thirties had come in like a hurricane. An entire young generation had been swept up in a violent protest against the realities of events. But the answers were numbing. The slogans were pieces of twine throttling something that was struggling. Phrases like "the toiling masses" did not answer terrible questions. There were always people, real people, each of them an individual spirit with its own peculiar past. The Spanish war was doubtless the last war in which individuals were to enter fully with their individual might. But what a welter of conflicting views this implies! The soldier is fighting not only *against* an enemy but also *for* some beyond.

But no war can be the purifying fire. Individuals cannot fight as individuals, and conflicting visions bring a conflict of will and design. Before I left Spain the disintegration had begun, with a squalid internecine brawl in Barcelona. I have never had much heart for party polemics, and it was not for factionalism that I had come to Spain. I did my best to find out "the facts"; I even went in May to Barcelona, where barricades were still in the streets. We shall never see that kind of outmoded fighting again. No more barricades! They were even outmoded then and proved nothing. I can't say to this day what really happened in Barcelona, in all the diversity of conflicting causations, but I do know for certain that it was no anarchist plot, hatched up in conjunction with Franco. If the enemies of Franco had split into groups and were killing each other, it was not because each group was not equally determined to defeat the common enemy. Was the aim of the war a revolutionary one, a strike at the terrible wrongs that had led to the uprising, or was it a "war for democracy," which, to the intransigents, implied no more than a restoration of the status quo? By that time, abstractions had taken over on the Loyalist side; on Franco's side, the superiority of weapons was surely winning.

My entry into the Hotel Florida in the heart of Madrid was surprisingly cozy. Hemingway came toward me in a kind of khaki uniform with high polished boots. I was dragging my knapsack; a white dust from shells exploding in the streets had coated my hair and felt gritty on my hands. He threw his arms around me and gave me a big kiss. "How are you, Josie? I'll never forgive you for letting that sixty-pound king off your line." Three years before, on a fishing trip in Key West with Hemingway and Max Perkins, I *had* let a kingfish get off my line, and secretly had been glad of it. Now here, in the Hotel Florida, in a war, was the fish, looking me in the eye. I didn't feel ashamed for my lack of skill; I had never set myself up as a fisherman. And at the moment I was grateful for the reference, which seemed to bring the world together and hold the disparate parts in conjunction. Hemingway was at home, if I wasn't, and that was something.

I don't know what the Hotel Florida had looked like before the war, but it now had a stripped appearance, with its bleak stuffed chairs abandoned in the lobby. On the clerk's desk was a little box with an invitation, TAKE ONE, and the one and only thing to take was a little brochure advertising the Hotel Plaza in Havana, Cuba. There was a lift, but to save the electricity it didn't run. I had a room on the fourth floor, and on that floor Hemingway had a suite of two rooms, one of which was occupied by Sid Franklin, his devoted friend and sort of *valet de chambre*. There was a tall wardrobe in Hem's room, and it was filled with tasty items: ham, bacon, eggs, coffee, and even marmalade. These tidbits were the fruit of Sid's ability to scrounge around, and as someone who knew Spain, had been admired in Spain as a valiant bullfighter, he could lay his hands on essentials no one else could have touched. As I was to find out, everyone hoarded a little of something. A few of the correspondents had even brought along little electric coffeepots. I had come in with a package of tea, some chocolate bars, and six packs of cigarettes.

As I think of the Hotel Florida now, I can see it only as a misty sort of unreality. I never seemed to be there, even when I was actually there. Something inside seemed to be suspended outside, waiting. Or listening. Or hovering around, in places where I had managed to be or in places that I heard of and to which I hoped to go. There was a disembodiment about my own entity, which didn't even disturb me. I soon got used to it. There was a kind of distinct core inside me, around which the disembodied elements might cluster as around a magnet, and they came and went around that magnet, sometimes swarming and buzzing. What I remember clearly was the way the floors opened up upon a deep well of a rotunda, so that walking around on your floor you could look down and see to the first floor, where people might be sitting, midgetlike, below.

After I had been to the front lines at Jarama, I used to sit there in the early mornings, when the boys on leave would have a chance to drop in to see me. I had my tea, and the only thing the hotel could furnish was hot water. With a bit of dry bread saved from supper the night before, I would sit munching and talking to the boys. Often Dos Passos was there doing the same thing. Then the odor of ham and coffee would slowly penetrate to our level, and from the fourth floor Hemingway would lean down and call, inviting us to breakfast. It was a terrible temptation. Everybody was hungry all the time, and smells incited to gluttony. I would be haunted all day, hating myself for being haunted. I hated it that I also felt virtuous for not going. For doing the right thing. For you couldn't run off from your visitors. Tomorrow they might be dead.

Though food was on everyone's mind, I never heard anyone complain of the lack of it or because some of the dishes served at the restaurant on the Gran Vía stank to high heaven. The restaurant was in the basement of a building nearly opposite the Telefónica, where you filed your dispatches and got permits for transportation. Gas was very limited, and it was hard to get a ride to anyplace. Hemingway had two cars for his use, with gas allowance, but then he was undertaking the movie *The Spanish Earth* and needed to be going back and forth to this village. It didn't always make for good feeling among some other correspondents, particularly those who were not on regular assignments and had only a short time allotted to them. I didn't feel so good myself seeing those cars go tootling off. Other people came out of the hotel and set off briskly, but where did they go? Martha Gellhorn sailed in and out in beautiful Saks Fifth Avenue pants, with a green chiffon scarf wound around her head. Everyone knew where he was going, what he was doing, except me. Everyone talked learnedly during the evening meal on the Gran Vía about the number of shells that had come in, the number of people killed. In a chaotic situation, to get hold of a few simple facts is consoling. If you can speak of them in terms of measurement, it is one way to control them. In Germany, during the inflationary period of the twenties, it had been the egg. I had lived with Germans in Berlin, and every day the egg was the center of conversation. "What is the egg doing today?" Why, the egg was a hundred thousand marks. Soon it was a million.

I had been assured at the press bureau that I would get to go places, but for days I was suspended, wondering, Where? In a situation like that it becomes second nature to hide one's ineptitude. You can't admit that you aren't bustling about, knowing exactly what it all means. If I had been a regular correspondent, I would have been obliged to show something for each day. But I was on a special kind of assignment, which meant I would write about other subjects than those covered by the news accounts. The people I wanted to know were the Spanish, but it seemed to me that I was out on a rim where the atmosphere often struck me as frivolous. There were some first-rate correspondents in Spain, and there were also some curious characters, like the journalist from England who had written a book about trawling. He had pale-blue eyes and pale hands that wandered helplessly over his food. If he caught me in the lobby, he would make an attack and fill me with factual information, none of which rang true. Or he would propound his sleeplessness. "I couldn't get to sleep last night. I kept thinking over and over: Out of the barbed wire of the war comes communism." Then he would stand back and wait for me to be electrified by his slogan. When I didn't electrify, he would trail off disconsolately.

I did a lot of walking around, looking hard at faces. There was nothing in shopwindows except a few sundrenched relics of other days. There was almost nothing to buy except oranges and shoelaces, and all this seemed wonderful to me. The place had been stripped of senseless commodities, and what had been left was the aliveness of speaking faces. The heavy shelling usually came in the afternoon, and if you got caught in it the only thing to do was to duck into some café. No one anywhere was well dressed, not even the tarts. There were no mantillas or black lace or shrinking girls with duennas. In the evening, on the way to the restaurant, the pavement was likely to be all hummocks and busted-up rubble. You picked your way with a flashlight. In the morning all this stuff would be swept up and new patches of cement would cover the holes. This went on, day by day, with the regularity of washing up the supper dishes.

I was just coming back from a stroll to the Puerto del Sol one morning when Sid Franklin called me from a little car. It stood in front of the Hotel Florida and held himself and Joris Ivens, who was shooting the film for *The Spanish Earth*. They were going to the village, and just out of the air, like manna from heaven, offered to take me along. Not to their village, but to Murata, the village near the front lines at Jarama. I jumped in just as I was.

Some of the fiercest fighting had taken place at a tangent up the Tajuña valley toward Murata not long before. The Fascists had made a dangerous push against the road to Valencia in January, and every available mixed brigade with its international troops had been rushed to the line. To have lost the battle would have been to seal the doom of Madrid, and there was no time to spare any man who could be thrown in. There were over four hundred Americans in the Abraham Lincoln Brigade, who had barely had time to learn to shoot a rifle or to handle a machine gun. Raw as they were, they went into the battle, and most of them came out alive. But shortly before I got to Murata, the Fifteenth Brigade had been ordered to launch an attack to take Pingarron Hill, the dominating terrain of the Tajuña valley. The attack had failed, and of the four hundred Americans, one hundred and eight were left.

The village of Murata didn't look like the center of a storm as we entered it. There was a town hall and a church and some empty spots filled with rubble, where houses had been. We passed through the town and began to mount into the hills. They stood in rounded hummocks or looked like jagged claws and seemed to be covered with an olive-colored pelt. Halfway up, we wheeled into the courtyard of what had been a farmhouse. A cart stood nearby, its shafts broken. There was a big wooden rake with a cat sitting under it. A rick of sodden hay was being pecked by a few straggling hens. The house was languidly open. Sunlight poured into plain whitewashed rooms where some cots were covered with neat blankets. No one was around. We could hear a murmur and, pushing on, entered a big kitchen. It had an enormous table, white as bone, and sitting at it were two young men in the cinnamon-colored uniforms of the International Brigade, peeling potatoes. The potatoes were very small and angry-looking and lay in a pallid earthy heap on the white table.

I said who I was, and fortunately the young men knew my name, mostly because of some articles I had written about Cuba. They didn't seem in the least surprised to see me there. They weren't even surprised when Joris and Sid simply drove off and left me. I offered to help with the potatoes, and they gave me a knife. We talked about the weather. There must have been some communication with brigade headquarters, in a big solid house not far off but hidden behind a hill, for in a little while a young man on a motorbike heaved into the courtyard and said I was to come with him to see the general. I had no notion then, nor have I now, whether he was a "good" general or a "bad" one. We spoke German though he was not a German; but neither was he a Russian. A Frenchman came in, spoke a few words, looked sharply at me, and went out. The general smiled, stamped a little card, and told me one of the boys would take me to the front lines. He hoped I would go. I could stay for a few days if I liked. It was fairly quiet now. They might order me out if things changed. But I could sleep at the little café in the village. One of the boys would see I got there.

It was too good to be true. From melancholic inertia, I felt I was walking on air. The young man with the bike walked back with me. A loud clatter came from the kitchen. They were chopping up onions. Then one of them brought around a tough-looking open car with good, heavy tires. On the way up the crooked road, the driver explained that this had been an old donkey road. They had leveled it out some to get supplies and an ambulance up to the men, but it was still bad. When we got to the top there would be a stretch of open ground we would have to cross before we came to the dugout leading to the trenches. The English battalion was to the right, and on the left were the Poles. There was a mixture of Spaniards in all of them, but it didn't always work out so well; they didn't like the same kind of food, for one thing.

Looked at from the top, the view was beautiful. You could see the town hall and the church of Murata, and you could see olive orchards and vineyards spreading softly along the hills toward the valley. The ground where there were no trees was harsh and brutally rocky. A man plowing in the distance was steering his plow as if it were a boat avoiding obstacles in a bay. The view in the other direction toward the front lines was wavery ground; many of the olive trees looked as if they had been split open with an ax. The inside pulp was pinkish and blue, with the look of quivering flesh. Blackened twigs lay scattered around the trunks. The ground itself had little plowed-up runnels that burst now and then into star-shaped pockets. I never saw this hilltop as a whole scene, but saw only its parts as they met the hurrying eye, because it took all of one's concentrated energy to get across this emptied space. The birds had deserted it. You could hear distinctly the rattle of a machine gun, then the olive tree near you shivered in a gust of wind. A bullet had passed by. Some leaves fell lightly. The thing to do was to walk swiftly toward your objective. We went in a straight diagonal without talking. Then suddenly we fronted an open dugout and dipped down to it.

A little group around a bare table with a telephone on it stared at us. The men had a wonderful red-brown color, and in their cinnamon-colored uniforms, with the baggy trousers gathered into stout boots, their youthful bodies seemed to have been fitted out with armor to mask their innocence. It is wonderful to have people glad to see you. These boys had been in the line for sixty days. It was by no means so tranquil as it seemed. They were expecting an attack anytime. To have a newcomer, not a soldier but a woman, suddenly pounce down into the dugout was a refinement of warfare they hadn't expected.

There was a camp cot, a cabinet with first-aid equipment, some chairs, and copies of a mimeographed sheet that they got out once a week. It was called *Mañana.* The boys had some hot coffee and gave me some. Even when we went along the line of trenches where soldiers were manning machine guns or lying beside rifles, I felt buoyant and, for the first time since I came to Madrid, not afraid. If you kept your head down, you were safer here than in Madrid so long as the attack hadn't begun. There was some firing all the time. But the front line of the enemy was very close, a few rods distant.

Boys who could not bear to shoot a rabbit back home had ancient guns that didn't work thrust into their hands on the night of the big offensive. Others tore the pins from grenades too soon, wounding themselves. Some went in with nothing but stones and tried to dig a shelter in the earth with cartridges. A wounded man might call only to the dead, who lay like shipwrecked sailors on the spurting earth. The nucleus of Americans left from the big offensive was holding tight together, but they must have felt, during the prolonged stalemate, where men died one by one, that the real war was going on elsewhere. Or that only the enemy would remember them and on some dark night swoop down and take them by surprise.

The long line straggled in a zigzag, and one morning I went up with two doctors to the British sector, where some of the men had refused to be inoculated against typhoid. The disease had broken out all along the line. The Americans had taken the shots without a murmur; the Poles stubbornly refused; even some of the British surprisingly resisted. The doctors were impatient and fearful of the typhoid threat. They thought the presence of a woman might shame the boys into submission. Sitting on a rock, I smoked a cigarette, while some twenty recalcitrant British soldiers filed out to a little plateau. It seemed to me an exposed position; you could hear the whine of bullets through the olive trees. The men were ordered to take off their tunics, strip to the waist, and the pale cage of their ribs looked pathetically vulnerable. The tanned faces, the ready-looking brown hands, didn't belong to the stemlike bodies, which held some of the translucency of the Indian pipe that grows only in dark woods. One of the doctors went into a routine pep talk and got out his needle. Some of the soldiers shuffled uneasily out of the line; others stood, hesitantly.

One of the younger men came toward me and, calling me "Doctor," began to tell me why he didn't want it done. At first he said his mother was against it. Then he admitted that the reason was that they were due to get out of the line. If they took the shot, they didn't know when they'd get out. They had already been in sixty days. They had been promised relief; it hadn't come. This was a kind of strike to get what had been promised. Then they had the notion that the shot would cripple their arms badly. Suppose you got a surprise attack? Suppose it was the Moors coming at you? Would you have a chance, hand to hand, with a bad arm? You always kept a bullet for yourself if it was the Moors. That was better than to let them get you and cut you up alive. All this was said quietly.

The boy had very blue eyes, and sometimes the eyes seemed to be laughing. I couldn't help but look at the pale bluish skin of his body, where the veins shone. It seemed to me the clothes were a masquerade and that he wore them as Indians might wear war paint. The cinnamon-colored uniform gave his body an appearance of health; underneath, the skin shivered with a kind of phosphorescent light.

If I sometimes felt that the scene where I stood or sat was a stage set due to vanish the next moment, it was because the players, with their sunburned faces, were the actors of the moment, who were concealing some of their real life in their role as soldiers. But none of them was trying to live up to any heroic image of the soldier; their modesty was one of their most engaging traits. They disparaged exaggerated reports of victories, which had been printed in the very papers that seemed to them pledged to nothing less than "the truth," and they warned me not to deal with blood-and-thunder stories. They could laugh at some of the letters from home while admitting it was wearisome to get repetitious slogans like the cries of cheerleaders roaring away to enhance a game they were not playing. And it seemed at the front that too little was done by the home-bodies in America, France, and England, who might have gone out on prolonged strikes to protest the infamous non-intervention pact or might even have dipped down more substantially into their own pockets. Doubtless many of the soldiers in the international line were under the old spell of "Workers of the world, unite," in the full belief that the true causes back of the war in Spain were revolutionary and that *this* time a great new world might once more have a chance. But the mirage of the future did not blind them to the present; it induced the opposite to an easy optimism. To be stupidly optimistic does not give courage; the longer you stand on the bank and tell yourself how brave you will be to swim the swollen river, the harder it will be to dive in. Someone might cite the story reported in one of the papers about the Cuban pitcher who was said to be throwing grenades into the enemy lines like baseballs, when the truth was he hadn't had a chance to get near enough to throw anything. What the Cubans had wanted to tell me was that once there had been sixty-four of them. Now there were twelve. Please to remember them. Remember Pablo Torriente Brau, a good newsman from Havana.

There were not only living soldiers in the little groups where we talked. The dead were present by their absence. The dead often seemed as real to me as the man who might be talking of his friend, the battalion adjutant, born in Tennessee, who never had raised his voice when he talked to the

146

men. Please remember Douglas Seacord. Remember Tomlison, who had commanded a machine gun company. Please remember. Not the dead as corpses, or even how they had died. But for the simplest ordinary things: for the way one rolled a cigarette or another had squatted in the dust to make good maps of their position with his finger. Or some man might suddenly want to talk about his little boy and how he stood in his crib, shaking the bars, laughing, and looking at his father, "just as if he knew me."

But as I was to find out, talk at the front was different from talk that might come from the same soldier once he was on leave in Madrid. At the front, he was pulled together, as if for a spring. He couldn't play around with his fears but had to keep them down, like the folded blades of a knife, deep in the pocket. So you also never heard much talk about military tactics, as you did among the noncombatants at the Hotel Florida, where there was a certain amount of vainglory in knowledge of the how and when. Nor did you get ghoulish accounts of the dead. What you sometimes got was a spurt of criticism of decisions, even open condemnation of some brash and willful leader. Privately, they even called one such man, who was sometimes headlined in heroic terms, "the murderer"; later, on the Teruel front, against orders, he actually led a little band into what turned out to be an enemy ambush and death.

We might even get on the subject of dreams, and leaning on his arm, a soldier with hazel eyes and an auburn cowlick would begin, "I had this funny dream," and then tell how he saw a wide river flowing into a bay. The water looked thick. It was lapping this rock, kind of. Then it seemed to be lapping at things floating in it. They looked like clots of something, old rags, kind of. Then he saw that the bay and the river were blood and the clots bodies. The bodies were dead. You could see the second it was over he was sorry he had told the dream; he fumbled in his breast pocket for something, and to take his mind off, I told him I dreamed of bread. It was true. At the Florida I was always having this dream of coming home from school and smelling my mother's wonderful homemade bread. In the dream I would head for the pantry and have time to lift the white towel from the beautiful golden loaves before I heard the thunder. I had to leave the bread to shut the windows so the rain wouldn't come in. Then I woke up. There was no bread and no thunder. Only the noise of the early bombardment.

They loved this story, and I had to repeat it several times. There may seem to be something childish in all this, but these were not childish men. It just happens that a kind of childishness, in the sense that the child knows how to savor joyful things, is a source of instinctual happiness, and even in this crucial situation, they had not lost the art or the heart for this kind of search. The Spanish soldiers had it to an even greater degree. When I saw them in their front lines at the Casa del Campo, they were often playing the fool.

The Hotel Florida was nothing at all after the front. The atmosphere at the restaurant on the Gran Vía was not exactly effete, and yet it now struck me as tiresomely superficial. There were little cliques, and it did not console me that characters who had paid no attention to me were now inclined to gather me to their bosoms because of what they considered my feat in establishing myself at Murata. At night I no longer dreamed of bread. My inner room looked out on a little well, and I could see shadows fall on the wall opposite when there was a moon. I longed for my room in Murata and its cold stone floor, where the chill shot up your leg like a toothache if you put your bare foot down. The shadows on this wall were barren; in Murata I could look out on the little empty street, where late at night a dog might wander or a single figure come to a doorway and stare up at the sky. When I thought of the long trench, the earthwork seemed like a wave that would be certain someday to fall. At the Florida, I would lie in my bed rehearsing the times I had walked through the trenches at Jarama. I could see the young Spanish boy leap to his feet with the cry *"Salud"* and watch other figures tidying up their little nooks as I approached. I could feel their hands, for to each you gave your hand as you passed by, and each hand was different. Some had a cool hardness; some clung, spasmodically tightening their fingers. If I had come like news of an outside world in which they still had a place because they were not forgotten, they reminded me of some inner necessity out of which I was struggling for some kind of answer. At the Florida, I could lie still, remembering some of their observations, which often had delicate poetic insights. I had looked over the top of the earthen wall, where the land rolled with the inevitability of a sea to that distant port which might disgorge some night the crawling creatures who came on their bellies like monsters of the deep. There was something primeval about my visions of that hilltop where the earth was often streaked with the slime of dead things. Then I would tell myself that this primeval world was in me, and that the boys on the line would bear up to the wave when it came better than I could.

All I wanted was to get out again, somewhere, to people who were "in it." Once more I had to wait. Others were also waiting in a state of discontent. A well-known journalist from London, with a pinkish dome around which were wound some miraculous wisps of pale hair as long as my arm, was obsessed with "atrocities." He had been in the Great War and had been a prisoner in Germany. There was an unhealthy glitter in his eyes as he told me that people rounded up as spies were shot regularly. He had been out to see the nicks in a high white wall against which they stood to die, and he had even surreptitiously counted the nicks. Dos Passos was worrying about his friend Professor Robles, who had translated his books into Spanish and who had been arrested as a spy, and Hemingway was worried because Dos was conspicuously making inquiries and might get everybody in trouble if he persisted. "After all," he warned, "this is a war."

Two of the boys from the Jarama front came to see me and, not finding me in my room, went to Hemingway's room, where they picked the lock of his wardrobe. They stole two jars of jam, which put Hemingway into a rage. The rage didn't mean a thing. Hemingway, like a good many others, was undergoing some kind of transformation, and part of the reason he had come to Spain was doubtless because the forces of that process were already at work. It wasn't only that he was giving up his wife for Martha Gellhorn. He had answered a definite call when he came to Spain. He wanted to be *the* war writer of his age, and he knew it and went toward it. War gave answers that could not be found in that paradise valley of Wyoming where he had fished or even in the waters of Key West when the tarpon struck. What was the deepest reality *there* was in an extreme form *here*, and to get it he had to be in it, and he knew it.

He was a real friend to the Spanish; he had donated an ambulance and had come as a correspondent. He was promoting the film *The Spanish Earth*, which was to show life in a village and what the war meant to the Spaniards. But in annexing new realms of experience, Hemingway was entering into some areas that were better known to people like Dos Passos or even myself. He seemed to be naively embracing on the simpler levels the current ideologies at the very moment when Dos Passos was urgently questioning them. On another level, Dos was absolutely right in refusing to believe that his friend could be guilty of treason; the bonds of friendship were not to be broken that lightly. You could feel the irritation growing between the two men and even wonder at the origin.

There was a kind of splurging magnificence about Hemingway at the Florida, a crackling generosity whose underside was a kind of miserliness. He was stingy with his feelings to anyone who broke his code, even brutal, but it is only fair to say that Hemingway was never anything but faithful to the code he set up for himself. He could give an ambulance but would not be able to stomach stealing jars of jam on the sly. It wasn't soldierly. When I laughed at the whole thing, he was indignant. Part of his exuberance came from the success of his love affair. But his love affair was not exactly a benign influence in a wartime hotel. The corks popping were not for you, and late at night on the stairs, after a trying day, some of the correspondents would be sitting talking about nothing much, just to put in time or to take the edge off jerky nerves. Now and then the divine odor of cooking would seep through the hallways, and Hemingway, bursting with vigor, would bustle around and confide in me that he had shot a hare and a partridge and that the good Spanish maid on our floor was cooking them for him. His feat would be presented as a virtuous act, and I was inclined to agree with him, even if I shared only the good smell. For as someone who could broil trout over a fire in the woods and had raised food in my own garden, I felt as he did, that there was a special virtue in the food that you had got together with your own hands. In the food line,

I would find myself compulsively narrating my own exploits. Our mouths would water.

There were days when you sat around brooding or lived only for that brief hour at noon when the bars opened for the sale of beer. Other days crammed the meaning of a lifetime into a few brief hours. One morning just before clear daylight I was awakened by two terrifying thuds. A heavy wall of water seemed to be crashing down with an iron force. But the havoc was in me, where the flood was swishing and my heart had become no more than a helpless chip. My hands shook as I tried to find my clothes; then I gave up and, throwing on a dressing gown, ran into the hall, where there was a strange sound like the twittering of birds at dawn in the country. People were running toward the rooms at the back, doors banged, and when Hemingway, fully dressed and fit, called out to me, "How are you?" I opened my mouth to say "fine," but no sound came. I rushed back to my room with the insane protest that had popped up—"But I didn't come here to die like a rat in a trap"—mocking me. For what had I come, if not possibly that? I managed to dress and to walk out again, and seeing Claude Cockburn with a coffeepot in his hand, walking with his head bent, pale but impeccable, I rushed up to him and took it from him.

We went to a room toward the front where the banging was heaviest. Thousands of rats seemed to be scrambling for their lives in the plaster of the walls. We got the coffeepot plugged in, but there was no coffee. Someone else brought coffee and someone else some stale bread. A toaster came from somewhere. Dos Passos, fully dressed and composed, even to a necktie, came in. A French correspondent in a vibrant blue satin robe emerged, carrying an armful of grapefruit, which he passed out to each of us, bowing to us in turn.

Who would give away precious grapefruit if this was not to be our last hour? No one ate the fruit, but each one, when the shelling was finally over, stole off with the loot. Hemingway blew breezily in and out. There was conversation, but I don't know what about. It was consoling to see everyone behave so well and to wonder if, within, the turmoil in others had been as hard to quell as it had been in me.

When the shelling was over, some people ran at once to the street. Hemingway came back with the report that the Paramount Theatre had got it, including the big sign advertising Charlie Chaplin's *Modern Times*. A team from England was out picking up shrapnel. An old man was displaying a handsome brass fragment that was clearly part of a German shell. A workman left his job of clearing up debris to join a little crowd that had gathered around him. The workman began to argue with him that it was his duty to give up his prize to the English to take back with them as propaganda. The English stood politely waiting. The old man was torn between duty and desire; one moment he held the piece out toward them, the next he drew it back. Then he fondled it and abruptly put it in his pocket, muttering that he had to show it to his daughter. The entire square was a mass of rubble of a pinkish-gray color that looked like the entrails of animals in an abattoir.

Though the day had barely begun, no one knew what to do with what was left of it. The big lobby was gritty with a pasty kind of sand. Some got consolation in talking about the merits of shelling as opposed to an air raid. Others analyzed the position of the hotel, which was in a suicidal spot, in the direct line of fire aimed at the War Ministry and the Telefónica. Though our lives had been spared, everyone was touchy. Hemingway asked me why I was so glum, and I answered angrily that I didn't feel like a Girl Scout and

I didn't care who knew it. Then he relented and invited me to his room for a snifter of brandy. But what he really wanted was to urge me to talk to Dos Passos and to tell him to lay off making inquiries about Robles. It was going to throw suspicion on all of us and get us in trouble. This was a war. Quintanilla, the head of the Department of Justice, had assured Dos that Robles would get a fair trial. Others in authority had told him the same. He should lay off. Quintanilla was a swell guy; I ought to get to know him.

His request was terribly disturbing. I had known all along that Robles had been shot as a spy. I had been in Valencia before coming to Madrid and there had been told, in strictest confidence, and for the reason that Dos Passos was an old friend of mine, that the man was dead. Some of the Spanish were beginning to be worried about Dos Passos's zeal, and fearing that he might turn against their cause if he discovered the truth, hoped to keep him from finding out anything about it while he was in Spain. I had no way of knowing whether Robles was guilty of the charges against him, but he had been in America, had been a professor at Johns Hopkins, was well known for his enlightened views, and there was the chance that he was the victim of personal enemies or even of some terrible blunder. The trouble was that I had sworn to keep this secret, just as my informant had been sworn by someone higher up. But the circumstances seemed to me more pressing than any promise. I could not believe Quintanilla so good a guy if he could let Dos Passos remain in anguished ignorance or if the evidence was so clear as not to admit contradiction. I felt that Dos should be told, not because he might bring danger down on us but because the man was dead.

So I put my drink down and said: "The man is already dead. Quintanilla should have told Dos." Hemingway was surprised. What were we to do? Because of my promise, I felt I should not be brought into it, but Hemingway might admit that someone had told him; someone from Valencia who was passing through but whose name he must withhold. Perhaps he agreed with too cheerful a readiness. I don't think he doubted for a minute that Robles was guilty if Quintanilla said so. But I did. Hemingway was to have an opportunity to talk to Dos that very day, for the three of us had arranged to go to brigade headquarters, where the Russians were installed. I had been fearfully curious, but now I wasn't even certain that I wanted to go. I didn't know how Dos Passos would take the news, and I dreaded to find out.

Rafael Alberti and his wife, Maria Teresa, were to go with us, and in fact had arranged the meeting, but probably because of my own state of mind, their ebullience, and their chatter, which went on with the vivacity of bright canaries, did not strike a sympathetic note in me. I felt I would rather read Alberti's wonderful poem "Sobre los Angeles" quietly at home than go twenty steps to meet him in his sparkling military boots and with his camera in hand, and his propensity for arranging groups for pictures, then leaping into the center of the group at the last moment while he thrust the camera into someone else's hand.

What I remember most, as we drove along the road through the countryside, was the sight of the Guadarrama Mountains, blue with purest white snow at the crown, and, beyond, a sky even more intense in its blueness. A bird, an actual bird, was flying above us, wheeling, and no words for it could be better than those written by the very man who was prattling away so volubly in the car that was taking us to the former castle of the Duke of Tovar.

> Se olvidan hombres de brea y fango
> que sus buques y sus trenos,
> a vista de pájaro,

son ya en medio del mundo una mancha de aceite,
limitada de cruces de todas partes.

Men of pitch and mud forget
That their boats and trains,
To a bird's eye,
Are a stain of oil in the middle of the world,
Bounded by crosses on every side.

No place could have seemed more remote from the
front than the castle when we drove past the big square
tower with its guard of soldiers and entered a patio where
the walls of the *alcaldía* were lined with shining blue-and-
white tiles and where big oleander trees in earthen pots were
spaced like sentries at regular intervals. When we went in
through an enormous kitchen, we seemed to have stepped
into a Brueghel painting; the coppery pans above the huge
fireplace—actual cooking was going on—seemed reflected
in the deeply sunburned faces of a dozen soldiers, who were
lifting spoons and forks around a table where dishes of food
sent up an appetizing steam. High windows let in sunlight
through delicate starched curtains that parted to show the
nodding tops of blooming lilacs.

It was as if we had stepped back into another age, where
only our oddly assorted presences served as dissonance. The
Russians had luncheon for us in a noble room where paintings of ancestors in ruffs and swords stared haughtily down
at us and where the Russians themselves, two attractive men
with soft voices, actually did not seem inappropriate substi-
tutes. The division commander, next to whom I was seated,
even spoke German, though I do not remember that I could
find anything that seemed worth saying. Most of the talk
was in French or Spanish, and though I knew from Dos

Passos's abstracted air that Hemingway had told him, he kept up his end of the conversation with considerable spirit. In the garden afterward, another officer, who had not been at luncheon, wanted to talk German with me, and though it was about world politics and the decline of capitalism, I felt I had heard all this before. With a little coffee cup in his hand, Dos came up to me and in an agitated voice asked why was it that he couldn't meet the man who had conveyed the news, why couldn't he speak to him too? The only thing I could think of was to tell him not to ask any more questions in Madrid. It would be better to wait until he got to Valencia and then see someone like Del Vayo and find out what he could.

Except for the chirping of Maria Teresa, who with coral earrings, a brooch, and a filmy scarf suddenly made me feel that I looked as austere as a nun, the ride back to Madrid was silent. Hemingway bolted from the car the second it landed at the Hotel Florida, and the Albertis shot off, leaving Dos Passos and me standing on the street, wondering what to do until it was time to pursue what would probably be a forlorn sausage stuffed with sawdust at the Gran Vía. Dos suggested we walk to the Place Mayor, which was part of the old but not a grand section of Madrid and which I did not know, although it was one spot that had been a favorite of his in other days. It wasn't far distant and was still beautiful. Some of the houses were mere shells, with the light from the setting sun illuminating their flushed skeletons. Houses with the top sliced off still held occupants, who continued to water the plants in the windows and to keep the bird cages, in which little birds were hopping and chirping, out in the open air.

But the best thing about the square was the horse. It was only a statue of a horse, but of such a spirited creature, with such a mighty tail and mane, that it suggested all the vitality of some great horse ancestor who had sired a race of triumphant winners. Its flanks glittered a coppery rose and upon its side had been painted in bold red the brand of the anarchist syndicate CNT. In the hand of the rider—for it had a rider, though of not so much distinction as the horse—had been thrust a little anarchist flag. A woman with eyes black as jet and with a knob of black hair throbbing at the nape of her neck leaned out a window. Some kids whooped from behind a pile of rubble. An old man, tilted in a chair against an empty shell, called out cheerfully: *"Salud."*

At the Gran Vía we had barely gone down the steps when the Englishman who had once been so happy writing about trawling came up to me and in a flutter said who did I think had arrived *now?* I was beginning to think he was like those factotums in Victorian novels who stand at the door of the ballroom and bawl out the names of the guests. Celebrities fascinated him, and he not only announced but foretold. He had foretold the arrival of a duchess and of a Lady Something-or-other. Now he was waiting to get my reaction to the Dean of Canterbury. "So he's arrived. What of it?" I said, knowing full well I annoyed. The trouble was that I had already cast my eyes on the black-frocked Dean, a well-meaning man, no doubt, with a large, pink, saccharine face, the head of a Humpty-Dumpty, bald and fringed with a little babyish skirt of lacy hair. His secretary was impounded on my floor and ran around in a long funereal skirt, with a bunch of keys dangling at her waist like some bailiff out of Dickens. No doubt about it, the day had brought out all my most contrary impulses. But I didn't get a chance to indulge them.

Sid Franklin on one side of me began to relate how he had come to be a bullfighter and that on killing his first bull he had puked. On the other side, the UP correspondent Hank Gorrel was reminding me that it would soon be the seventeenth day of heavy shelling and that the press bureau might have to move from the Telefónica. The evening ended at a movie with Hank. It was Marlene Dietrich in a spy movie, and the glamorous creature was finally led out to be shot. Perhaps back home it might have gone down, but here in the heart of Madrid, with shells beginning to crash down once more and some people rushing out, others hissing *shush*, and angry calls to the back, where a big black curtain was carelessly left open by somebody hastily exiting, the whole drama was hilarious. We laughed until the tears came. "What a production!" Hank exclaimed. "How could anyone in their right minds think they could get away with it?" Then he went on to say, soberly, that war was a production, and he feared that he had been typed as a war correspondent. This was the third time he had been shot into a big production, and if you asked him, we were only seeing, here, a prelude to the biggest smash production of all.

In Madrid it began to seem more and more a tight squeeze, and though it was actually a front, with the lines not far off in the Casa del Campo, it often seemed utterly remote from the more meaningful scenes you might witness in the villages. For in Madrid, no matter what you might see or where you might go, you were obliged to rotate around the axis of the Florida and the Gran Vía, and with characters coming and going, even to a movie actor from Hollywood, the atmosphere began to feel, as the correspondent with the pink dome confided to me, "more and more like Bloomsbury." But for all that, individuals went about their business soberly, and Herbert Matthews, of the *New York Times*, not only kept to the line of duty but strolled around, discovered tiles that had been designed by Goya taken from a wrecked mansion, and began patiently to collect a few. When you passed Hemingway's room, you heard the busy sound of his typewriter pecking away.

As for myself, I soon found out that the first requirement was not to make a nuisance of myself or to press for any privileges, but the odd thing was that this very condition seemed to invite the miraculous chance. Even Pink Dome went out of his way to invite me along after he had wangled a car to drive to a village where raw Spanish troops were being drilled in three columns up and down the street. The trumpeter who set the signals was very young and handsome, in a red shirt with the neck open and short sleeves and wearing a cap cocked to one side above stiff curls that might have belonged to one of those carved wooden angel Gabriels that I had once admired in the medieval churches in Germany. The troops were tagged out in all sorts of costumes; smocks, old ragged shirts, faded corduroys or old frayed pants, but they marched with a proud pomp that brought praise from Pink Dome, who fancied himself as something of an expert from the Great War and insisted on peering down the barrels of their guns, which he pronounced clean but in need of oil. One of their officers, also in ragged pants, said there wasn't any more oil. But when the trumpet blew, the men marched with fine straight backs, proud swinging steps, while their leaders, brisk and happy, watched to see what Pink Dome might say. At the bugle call to halt, they all stopped on the instant, wheeled on a dime, and were pronounced by the British expert to be excellently disciplined.

I was more interested in them when they were at ease or loafing amiably inside a church, where the altar now held an assortment of kits hanging by straps and ammunition, and where a horse—a horse!—turned a powerful neck from munching hay to stare at us with mild eyes. There was a big iron kettle outside, from which the men were ladling stew, and they even offered us some. It tasted better than anything we got at the Gran Vía, as seemed only fitting. Not far away, in another village, the same thing was going on, and this time the men were exercising on what had been a threshing field, which still held the firm beautiful color of a golden loaf of bread. As they wheeled and turned in the lovely ambient air, the blue and red of their smocks bellied out with the exuberance of little flags. All the color seemed to have drained upon the field, which sparkled with gold and blues, reds, and greens and made the womenfolk, some of whom stood watching on the sidelines, seem like little black withered fig trees. But that was only the superficial view, for though they were in the perpetual black clothes of women always in mourning or always at work, their eyes snapped with an inner fire.

More than once I wondered at what we had assumed to be the vaunted independence of the American woman: when I saw the proud authority of the Spanish woman, upheld by something more than reliance upon any external-ity; or—as on the night I stayed in the caves above Alcalá de Henares, where the old, the children, and a few of the less able-bodied women remained during the day while the rest trudged down the steep mountain to work in the fields even when they were under fire—when I saw women of sixty come proudly home, erect, magnificently wrathful as they shook their fists at far distant towers of enemy smoke piercing the sky, or burst out into gorgeous obscenities oddly mixed with symbolic religiosity, which reduced my memory of fashionable ladies back home, with their little stereotyped lavender curls and their mincing high heels, to a parody of a potential they had forfeited.

In that ancient cave that the Moors had carved so fabulously out of living rock, the people of the ruined Alcalá de Henares had set themselves up, each in his little household, and at night songs echoed along the corridor as they cooked suppers over tiny fires. A baby had been born the day before I was there, and lay in a little crypt with his mother on a mound of hay covered with a worn blanket. He was very tiny and looked in his new raw redness more like a little image carved from wood than an actual child. The entire community was proud of his arrival, as if he had been blessed by fire and would certainly survive to reap the benefits of their struggle. Though there was ominous foreboding elsewhere, which events were to confirm, among the people of the villages you got nothing except the will to win. Those who didn't want to win had run away or were concealed in some hypocritical setting, biding their time.

But there were times when I sometimes wondered how much they actually relished the presence of so many foreigners, even though they were soldiers. The Spaniard is so proud, and so deeply self-reliant, that it must also have been a wrench to be brought to a pass where outside help was needed. There were conflicting reports about the reaction among Spaniards to this foreign invasion, and there is no doubt that it differed with different communities. The soldiers of the International Brigade had great delicacy in handling the situation in the little towns near which they were billeted, and often found the simplest ways to win the confidence of some townsmen, who in turn might win over all the rest.

I know that once, when I had managed to get myself transported to the little village where they were making *The Spanish Earth*, and the others had driven away and left me, I felt it was outrageous that I should be willing to linger to eat into the villagers' scant supplies. For food was so precious, and it would have been different if I could have come without empty hands. On that day, once I was alone, I wandered along the little street, where some of the houses had been flattened in earlier air raids and which seemed so empty because every able-bodied man was at the front and the old men and most of the women were in the fields working to cultivate the crops. At the edge of the village a few goats were cropping the scant grass and the children were gaily playing a game that looked like drop-the-handkerchief. Only it was a little rag. I sat down and idly took out a notebook in which I often made little sketches of the terrain. There were some nearby hills that looked shaved off, and in their flattened sides were holes that might have been made by some gigantic bird and that reminded me of the swallows that used to build in the clay banks along the Missouri in Iowa. Little flowers grew modestly, in a scratchy sort of way, and I picked a few, pressing them in the notebook. But I had not been long, idly sketching and mostly to compose myself while I figured out what to do, when I felt the presence of somebody and, looking up, saw that a circle of children had gradually drawn near me and were watching me intently. One small boy had so beautiful a head that I found myself trying to draw it, and when a little girl edged near me, she screamed out that it was Pedro! I was flattered that she could see a likeness, and before I knew it, I was taking orders from them and they in turn were ordering each other to stand in line and "to be next." It was like a funny kind of photograph gallery and with such gusts of laughter, and even mockery at my failures, that before I knew it I had let them marshal me around the village, where nothing would do but that I "do" old Uncle Ramón, who was huddled in his chair in the sun, and then go after Grandma, whose hands were deep in the washtub.

It ended by my staying in the mayor's house for a few days—the mayor was of course at the front—and going with his wife to pick up twigs to make a fire to cook with. There was literally nothing to make a fire with except clippings from grapevines, which were hoarded like precious jewels in a sort of casket of dried branches. Someone had killed a goat a short time before, and it was delicious cooked in olive oil with garlic over a tiny fire of twigs. As for eggs, the mayor's wife and I trudged all around the village to collect a few and even went to those holes in the hillside that looked as if made by huge birds, where people lived in caves hollowed out and where some old woman, standing at the door, would advise us to hang around a few minutes, as the hen was on the nest and would be off shortly, with an egg for us. The nest would be within the whitewashed den, which was kept neat as a pin and had been scooped out in such a way as to catch the warm rays of the sun. There would even be a goat making himself at home alongside the hen, or a homely donkey amiably coming up to look over the newcomers.

Caves like these were not just wartime provisions but features of a country where the lifeblood had drained down a few funnels to the rich. The owner of the manor had fled to Franco, leaving his wealth of grapevines, which it was the duty of the villagers to cultivate for his profit. That he had abandoned the village did not mean they were to abandon the vines, and they had harvested the grapes, sold them in the usual way, and bought a pump with the proceeds, which was to pump the waters of the river to an area of land that might be irrigated to make the gardens the villagers had never had. They were at this work now, and the seeds had already been planted, the little life-giving rivulets were watering onions, melons, and vegetables that some of the kids of the village had never so much as tasted.

One night, driving out from Madrid to the Guadarrama under a quarter moon, which was the only light allowed, I had a chance to see what pains some of the soldiers of the International Brigade took to reconcile the villagers to their presence. Not a chink of light shone from the squat dark houses, and our feet rattled noisily as we walked over the rough cobbles and opened a door. A battery crew of Germans were eating supper on a table spread with a white cloth. Pitchers of wine glowed under the beaded lamp, which swung from a useless chandelier, now shrouded carefully in green netting. They were all hard at work on a platter of eggs, with coffee in pink cups steaming beside their plates. The faces had a curious uniformity: I can only describe it by saying that they looked confident and joyful. One has to remember that these men had been summoned, as it were, from the shadow of a cellar. The whistle that the very air gives to every child at birth had been stopped up with dirt. Now they had cleaned the whistle, and whether for a little while or for years they might be allowed to make the music of the living didn't perhaps matter so much to them as the fact of the *now*, which had restored them to visibility where they were actual men. They were no longer like sleepwalkers whose actions are mechanical and meaningless and who are haunted by menacing noises and phantoms of the dark. Inescapable as their private troubles may have been, *here* at least, as if they had been on shipboard sailing from port to port, they could do nothing about them, and the saving grace was to use the *now* as if it were literally the forever.

So it is not so farfetched to say that this one evening had a celestial quality and that the little girls of the village, in their skimpy white dresses, sang like angels. Or that the schoolroom packed with many different nationalities had the benign air of those paintings called "The Peaceable Kingdom," made by the Quaker Hicks in Pennsylvania when he was trying to reconcile the animal world to the human, the invading whites to the Indians, and painted the Lion lying down beside the Lamb. If the soldiers' chorus of Yugoslavians, with their leader rounding his O's and leaning forward with his hand transformed to a baton, reminded me of the frescoes in Italy where Fra Angelico's band of musicians resembled the choirboys who sang in the big cathedral, it was because everything during this evening reminded me of something else, and that something always vibrant and living. It was a kind of enchanted world, which was being kept suspended, like the colors in a soap bubble that may burst all too soon but while it lasts reflects in gorgeous illusion every smallest object in the little universe where it will soon explode to nothing.

There was even an accordion solo—"Solo Mio," of course—and a German recited a long narrative poem, filled with witty idiomatic allusions that nobody could understand except the Germans. But everybody applauded like mad, and a mother stoppered up her bawling kid's mouth with a wine-soaked hunk of bread, which he blissfully chewed. The Czech soldiers sang Goethe's "Röslein, Röslein, Röslein Roth" with the tenderness of men who were actually serenading a real sweetheart, and the evening was pitched so high that when the clown burst out, with a face whitened by flour and a pink skirt over his uniform, dangling a silly pocketbook from a stout wrist, it was almost unbearable. The audience moaned with pleasure. People at the back of the room clambered up on their chairs. Someone fell with a squeal. It took a lot of shushing and hissing to quiet people down so they could listen to the violin solo played by a handsome Hungarian who had been the first violin in the Budapest orchestra, followed by two comic Romanians, stamping and singing—of all things—"Who's Afraid of the Big Bad Wolf"!

Afterward we went to another house, where the girls of the village had arranged roses and ferns in a little silver dish for the center of the table and where the soldiers, pressing around, produced a few bottles of champagne. Then they brought out photographs of groups taken with different nationalities all congenially intermingling, as if the photographs could substantiate forever the hope they had tried that evening to sustain. The Germans made me accept packages of Lucky Strikes, inasmuch as they insisted I "belonged" to them because I knew through my own skin what Germany had come to be like.

My room at the Florida was hardly bearable when I got back to it, and it was all I could do to keep from opening the door and shouting "Dry up" at the little group on the stairs who were intoning monotonously: "I've been working on the railroad/All the livelong day."

If the next morning was so quiet that everyone at lunch at the Gran Vía had relaxed to an almost ordinary temper, the peace was short-lived. I was about to leave the restaurant when Hemingway called me to his table, where he was sitting with Virginia Cowles, who was there for King Features, and Pepe Quintanilla. When I heard his name, I looked hard at him, as the man who had not told Dos Passos the truth about Robles, but his looks were as disarming as anyone's looks can be. In the old days he would have been called a police officer, but now he was head of the Department of Justice, and the question was, Could any court actually dispense justice? So I sat down, a little gingerly, as he went on with some amusing tidbit about Spanish artists in Paris, who in the good old days had hung around La Rotonde and had a little factory, painting Grecos by the yard for rich South Americans. They have five times stolen blocks of building stone to lug home to turn into sculpture.

The next second he was talking about Maneas, the anarchist miner, who had simply taken a butcher knife on one of the first crucial days, when they hardly had anything to fight with, and calling to the members of their little group—who were lying low on the roof and whom he had accused of being intellectuals who would never fight—yelled: "Come along, you bastards," and, running straight at the enemy, had fallen with a bullet in his chest. But it was his kind, said Quintanilla, who had saved the day in Madrid, by calling upon everyone to do the impossible. Crazies, crazies, he repeated, smiling and shaking his head. There were lots of crazies. Sometimes kids. Like the time twenty soldiers ran out of ammunition and sent the kids back for it, and when the kids brought it back they refused to give it up. The men had to fight the kids to get it and then fight the enemy. Crazy. There was the lieutenant who wouldn't give up his three bars for the one due him as a newly made captain. What, give up three for one! Nothing doing. Of course, he couldn't read or write. In Spain that's one great trouble. At this point a shell fell and sounded as if it had dropped right outside the restaurant. Quintanilla kept on talking, telling little stories, but each time a shell fell, he counted. By the time he came to ten—interrupting what he said each time to count—he was flushed and the rest of us had become very quiet. The lights in the restaurant were lowered, and everybody except those at our table left. Even the waiters left. By the time Quintanilla had counted fifteen, they all came back, for some reason or other, standing around near the door to the kitchen.

We suddenly find we have no more cigarettes. A waiter leaps forward and offers Quintanilla the last of his tobacco out of a pouch, pouring it into a paper and rolling it carefully. Quintanilla's fingers, as he takes the thin cigarette and puts it in his mouth, are delicate and transparent-looking. The shoulders of his coat are awkwardly padded, his hair is thinning, but his gray-green eyes not only are completely alive but can emit warm sparks.

"I only carry one card, to permit me to ride on a streetcar," he says. "Sixteen. The rest I keep concealed in an inner pocket. At home there are eight guards. I know how men die, all right. It's worse if it has to be a woman. Seventeen. One officer shat in his pants, huddled in a corner. He had to be carried out, to be shot like a dog. Eighteen."

Hemingway interrupts and says he has got to go.

"Nonsense," says Quintanilla. "No one goes."

"*El Rubio,*" says Hemingway quietly, thinking of Martha, back at the Florida.

"Nonsense," repeats Quintanilla.

"Work, I must work," says Hemingway, half out of his seat.

"Crazy, crazy, no," says Quintanilla, and beckons to a waiter to bring cognac. When it comes, he pours some for everyone, and the waiters, standing near the door, who seem to have been waiting for this, bolt their drinks and then vanish.

"There is no work once you get hit," says Quintanilla. He turns toward Virginia Cowles, who has been sitting quietly but looks very pale. A little blue line shows around her mouth. She is young and pretty; dressed in black, with heavy gold bracelets on her slender wrists and wearing tiny

169

black shoes with incredibly high heels. I often wondered how she navigated over the rubble from the Florida to the Gran Vía. Now he pats her knee reassuringly and says: "We will all go to my house. I will divorce my wife and marry you. There are plenty of beds, plenty of room, even for Hemingway, an old man who is still green."

"I am only thirty-eight," says Hemingway.

"An old man but still green," insists Quintanilla. Then he takes out a picture of his son and shows it proudly. "I have a son," he tells Virginia, "and you won't have to make another. Just be my wife. My wife can be the cook. I have lived with her so long that it is just like mailing a letter, and my only worry is will the stamp get on."

"Your wife is a magnificent woman," says Hemingway.

"We will kill a sheep and have wine. We can have a fine time. You can be the lover, and I'll be the husband. Twenty-five."

"I'm afraid when you get tired of me you'll make me be the cook," says Virginia. We all burst into laughter, happy to hear our voices.

"I think it is letting up," says Hemingway. "I've got to go."

"No," says Quintanilla. "Twenty-seven." The plaster has been tinkling rather pleasantly, like ice in glasses, inside the walls. Above, a big window crashes. Twenty-eight. Then comes a long pause, and we all get up and gingerly go up the basement stairs leading to the street. It looks fuzzy, in a fume of cloudy dust from where the explosions hit, and empty, except for two soldiers with a girl between them, humping along, arm in arm, down the middle of the street, over the hunks of rubble, through the steamy rose-tinted mist. Quintanilla pokes his head out, screaming: *"Hombres,*

hombres, go back, keep away. Go back." But the *hombres* pay
no attention to him and crookedly, as if they are drunk,
zigzag arm in arm, where not a hundred feet ahead of them
a shell suddenly cracks down, sending up a cloud of steamy
dust and a clatter of falling stones. "Crazy, crazy," moans
Quintanilla. "Simply crazy. It happens like that. They walk
right into it. Wait, we must wait."

We went below again and waited some more and by
this time no one counted and the stories had ended. "If we
only had a cigarette," said Quintanilla. Then we got up once
more and decided to chance it. The street was murky and
plowed; a little man in a white apron was out with a bucket
of water and a broom, grimly washing up a big pool of
blood. Even our hotel had got a direct hit this time, and the
balcony had been chipped off. But no one had been killed.
A nervous aviator from the front said he wished he were
back in his little two-seater.

Some correspondents were going to take a leave to
England. New ones arrived. H. L. Brailsford from London,
whose writings I had long admired, came and sat like a little
gray chipmunk waiting for a car to take him places. One of
the Hungarian commanders came from the front, bringing
a ham in a tin and packs of Camels, and suggested that we
buy champagne. But when Sid Franklin stuck to us like a
burr he ordered wine instead. Then they got into an argument. The Hungarian called bullfighting a barbaric business. Sid said it was an art, a great spectacle when well done,
and he earned much money at it. "And what about your
opinions?" asked the other. Until he came here, he had never
been interested, Sid explained. Now he was trying to make
up his mind.

"You ought to let it go," said the Hungarian. "It's too
late to make up your mind."

"If the Fascists win, it will put us back a thousand years," said Sid.

"If you have got that far, how can you stop? The bull-fight is a sham fight. You should fight in this war in a great cause. The important thing is a *Weltanschauung,* but for that we pay. One pays for everything. For *everything.*" He seemed to have turned to stone and sat cold and stoic, staring at the table.

With his eyes on the ham, Sid whispered to me, asking me if he could buy some of it. I looked at him in astonishment and began to laugh. "Are you crazy? Of course not." More than once Sid seemed to rub someone from the front the wrong way. But there was no one at the Hotel Florida who did more to keep up morale, just by a kind of buoyant mindlessness that was wonderfully contagious. He could smile when everyone else was glum or crack a joke or bargain for perfume or jewelry to take back home in a little shop where the shopkeeper might bring out a hoard of treasures that no one else was ever allowed to see. He couldn't understand why I wouldn't invest in furs. "You'll never get such a bargain again," he insisted, and made me go to a shop where the owner dug out some beautiful skins that were of the unborn lamb. "Just look how they shimmer," Sid said. "Beautiful. And wonderfully cheap." He couldn't understand why I didn't even want them. "I couldn't" was no answer for him.

He even liked to get off cynical remarks in front of some of the boys from the Jarama front, who might have only one evening in Madrid and must sometimes be thinking that evening might be their last. A kind of nervous anxiety had overtaken them; they were almost longing for the dreaded attack. One night Sid was rattling away about women and saying that sex was no more than a drink of water. "Take it or leave it," he said airily. He could be funny, too, about the rounding up of the whores, and that one of them had been sent scuttling from the hotel with her pajamas in a paper bag. But this particular girl was one that everybody liked; one of the boys from Jarama even tried hard to imagine that he had fallen in love with her. He felt it was unjust that the girls should get it in the neck; that they should be treated as spies without any difference made between those who might be and those who were loyal. Somehow he had imagined that here, of all places, things would be ordered differently.

Sid's contention that what everybody wanted was security didn't go down well either. "It's not true," one of the Jarama men whispered to me. "What they want is happiness. And something to believe in." But the word "happiness" confused him, even pained him. He squeezed his eyes shut and asked me if I would walk out with him. "I need air," he said.

This fellow was in a position of command, but my lack of interest in military details kept me from even noting what his distinction was. He wore the same uniform as everyone else, but he was responsible for a good number of men, and it was the men, who "were like children and looked to him," who were now on his mind. "Someone gets it every day or so. Just a nick here, a nick there. They look to me to see what to do. I don't know what to tell them. The lines are so close. They'll attack with grenades sooner or later. Or we will."

Then he dropped it and took up Sid. He didn't like that kind of talk; all that drink-of-water stuff. He had loved his wife. "You should see my kids, a girl and a boy." But he didn't know when he would ever see them, or what they would be told about him if he was killed, for his wife had left him.

We began to walk, and somehow the talk about the boys in the Jarama line and his wife waiting for her kid to be born all got mixed up together. The night in the trenches while they waited for an attack seemed like a hideous counterpart to the night when his wife had waited for the doctor who didn't come. When she had the girl, she had gone to the hospital, but with this one, hard times had struck. He got paid in paper scrip that no one wanted. There was a doctor lined up, but when her water bag burst two weeks ahead of time, they couldn't get hold of him. In the middle of the night, they were all alone, with her pains coming hard. She gripped his hands so tight that he could feel it to this very moment. It was so dark; he kept looking out the window. His eyes just gnawed the dark, trying to make a hole for the doc to get through. He tried to get another doc, but there wasn't time. Time—it squeezed you up and wrung you dry and limp. Then she said, I can't help it; it's coming. He rushed to wash his hands. Then he thought he heard a step and ran to the door, but no one was there. Then the boy came. A fine fellow. He tied his cord. When it was all over, both doctors came. One was smoking a big cigar.

I had stumbled over a pit in the pavement; when he caught hold of my hand, his own was wet. I could not see his face, only feel how he felt and that he was sorting things out from a jumbled mass of experiences if only to make some order to help him to live. Did I remember that fellow at the front, the dark guy with a cut on his cheek? He had been killed, and it was an awful thing to say but it was a kind of relief. You know what? He actually liked to kill, and it was all they could do to keep him from killing the prisoners they sometimes brought in. Why, that fellow would actually cry, and bite his hand until the blood came, and say, But it's so nice! Can you beat that? Some of the prisoners might be giving themselves up, and just hoping we would catch them. A Spaniard knew one such man who had been brought in. They had come from the same village, and he knew it was true that this fellow had been trapped by the Fascists and forced to fight for them. This prisoner said there was a lot of discontent in their lines; and they only got meat once a week. Why wouldn't there be discontent? You couldn't tell him that the ordinary guy wanted to see Franco win. Look who ran after him. The rich. Had I seen any of those big houses? Some of the wounded boys were convalescing in them. Wonderful joints. But what could the owners be like when they had these photographs stoked away in some little drawer, bunches of them, of some swell dame that one of the Spaniards said was a fashionable duchess, taken stark naked with a naked man, and in poses you'd never expect to find except on those dirty postcards they were selling you in Paris.

Or sometimes late at night, sitting on the stairs at the Florida, talking to whoever might be there, we would be interrupted by the rap of high heels and see some of the "girls" being herded along the hall. "Just when she was giving a little comfort to some poor guy," remarked one of the men.

Though spies began to be on everyone's mind, no one could imagine who they might actually be. You never saw one. The "girls" locked up for a night would be certain to filter back, if not at the Florida, then elsewhere. But I noticed, when we made trips out of the city and our car was stopped for the password, that the only papers they were interested in were mine, as the one woman present, and that when on the first of May they stopped the car and poked a head inside to look carefully, saying, "The first of May," our prompt answer, "Unite and fight," the password for the day, satisfied them about everybody except me. They had no suspicions about me except that I was a woman, and as such a possible threat. But what concerned me was that I was a noncombatant, and as such I was probably due to move on. I even told myself that I was eating too much, though it was very little and I had lost twenty pounds.

Unite and fight seemed so terribly urgent that no one could believe the news from Barcelona. What? Barricades? With Loyalists fighting their brother Loyalists and not Franco? But some of the correspondents had warned all along that even if Franco won, a civil war was certain to follow. There were rumors and counterrumors. H. L. Brailsford was stunned, and as he had more background than almost anyone else, it was a comfort to talk with him. He agreed that when you are at war with a deadly enemy it is better not to begin fighting among yourselves, yet said it is well to remember that it takes two to make a quarrel and that people do not begin building barricades unless they have received something that they regard as provocation. The Spanish anarchists had been persistently denigrated in the foreign press for some time, and he intended to go to Valencia and look up some of his friends among the anarchists and get to the bottom of it. The war had come to a point where the anarchists were probably asking questions. Were they fighting for the same old stuff or for a redress of ancient wrongs? When I asked him if he believed what they were putting out about POUM, he shook his head. "It sounds bad," he said. "That's one reason I can't believe it." But when I cornered Claude Cockburn, whose paper, *The Week,* had always had so much information no one else carried that even prime ministers took it, he could only shrug and say: "They are putting out the usual line of accusations; they claim they've got documents to prove collaboration with Franco."

When Brailsford told me he had wangled a car and if I wanted to go with him to Valencia to come along, I was ready to go that instant, if only because I didn't want to say any goodbyes. Except for one more item, I wrote no more in my journal. But I couldn't resist putting down a conversation at a little filling station halfway to Valencia, where a young Spanish officer came up to the car and, beaming, asked me if I did not remember him. The day I had been at Guadalajara and looked through the periscope? It was on a day when I had visited the German battalion and had deployed through a beautiful field to climb a whaleback mountain, on top of which a lookout had been established. From that point you could see directly opposite across the valley to another whale with gun emplacements and another lookout—the enemy—doubtless looking at you. It had so innocent a look, enhanced by the sound of a gramophone playing some lighthearted music, that you couldn't believe that this terrain, sprinkled with tiny delicate flowers, was a deadly place, which would be paid for, inch by inch, with human lives. The young officer had been in charge of the lookout, and now he was being sent to a school for more training. He was happy and proud. As we were talking, a simple townsman came up and listened in, enchanted. "A commander?" he questioned the young officer, politely. As there were women soldiers in Spain, it was not so strange a question as it seems. "No, no," answered the officer in a low, intimate voice. "American?" The officer nodded, and we went on talking about his school. When he spoke to me he raised his voice as one does to the deaf. It is the way people do to someone who is not completely conversant with the language. The townsman was beaming and listening with all his might. Once more he plucked at the soldier's sleeve. "But she understands everything!" "Everything," repeated the soldier, condescendingly. *"Muy inteligente."* *"Valiente,"* breathed the small townsman. *"Muy valiente."*

But I was far from understanding everything. About the most important questions, at that moment, I felt sickeningly at sea. As for being *valiente,* who wasn't? If I wrote it down in my journal, it was to put heart in myself, if only to say, Come now, be *muy inteligente,* be *valiente.* Just try.